Pr 

and *Negotiate Like A CEO*

The best there is. Literally.

Boris Feldman, Head of US Technology Practice, Freshfields Bruckhaus Deringer

Jotham has helped me throughout my career, from setting up strong employment agreements to securing stock compensation to protecting the management team during the sale of my company. Jotham is a guy you want in your corner. His book should be required reading for any exec who thinks 'this could never happen to me.'

Andy Cohen, founder and former CEO, Caring.com

As a hi-tech Silicon Valley attorney, Stein is brutally honest in assessing a situation and advising his clients. In *Negotiate Like a CEO* you'll learn to be aware, to recognize potential employment pitfalls, and how to protect yourself. You'll also learn that you may have more leverage than you might think, either now or as you advance in your career.

Grady Harp, Amazon Top 100 Hall of Fame Reviewer

As a CEO and multi-time Silicon Valley executive, I was very fortunate to learn from Jotham early in my career the great importance of the protective employment offer letter. Employment law is very complex and with this book you can learn from the best.

Bonnie Crater, co-founder and CEO, Full Circle Insights; former SVP salesforce.com; former SVP Genesys; former VP Oracle; former VP Netscape

I've been through changes in management, company sale, company relocation, downsizing and working for out and out a–holes. I had thought that I had agreed to some good offer letters and separation agreements over the years. In retrospect, I found that I left so much on the table and was vulnerable in many areas. This book is for us lowly peons who never made it to the C-Suite.

John Lotito, Former Chief Information Officer at several companies

I relied on Jotham when I was an exec at public companies – now my business relies on him to help it grow. Best lawyer for execs and entrepreneurs I know.

Michael Archer, CEO Common Interest Management Services; former SVP, Dun & Bradstreet; former President and CMO, Corporate Executive Board (now Gartner)

Jotham is a very valued legal adviser who also provides broad and pragmatic business guidance to our medical clinic and has for years!

Gregory Buncke, M.D., Director; The Buncke Clinic

Jotham has been invaluable to me for decades in critical areas such as employment agreements and company acquisitions.

Scott Eagle, co-founder and CEO, MDM Enterprise Solutions, Inc.; co-founder and former COO, 12 Digit Marketing, Inc.

Negotiate Like a CEO isn't afraid to share the cold, hard facts of the business world and give you the real guidance you need.

Rachel Song, Editor and Writer

Negotiate Like a CEO provides the ultimate no-nonsense guide for those who want to protect themselves, their friends, and family, both in the business world and personal life. It doesn't matter how big or small your company or dreams are, this book is one you must read. Highly recommended.

Susan Keefe, Midwest Book Review

Negotiate Like a CEO is a tremendous resource and a book you must read if you aspire to be successful in business. Highly recommended.

John J. Kelly, Detroit Free Press

NEGOTIATE LIKE A CEO

How to Get Ahead with Lessons Learned From Top Entrepreneurs and Executives

Jotham S. Stein

Political Animal Press
Toronto • Chicago
www.politicalanimalpress.com

Distributed by the University of Toronto Press
https://utpdistribution.com/

Cataloguing data available from Library and Archives Canada

ISBN 978-1895131-59-8 (paperback)
ISBN 978-1895131-60-4 (ebook)

Typeset in Adobe Garamond, designed by Robert Slimbach and Brandon Grotesque, designed by Hannes von Döhren.

Printed and bound in Canada.

To my mother, Pearl
And to her three siblings who are no longer with us,
Sarah Hack, Oscar Grubert, and Harry Grubert

Contents

Lessons: List of Entrepreneur and Executive Stories

1

Introduction – Negotiate Like a CEO

This book will help you protect yourself in employment, or if you're an entrepreneur, in your relationship with the company you founded.

Why do you need protection?

Because people just like you get fired! Yes, just like you! They get fired all the time! It doesn't matter whether you are a regular employee, a manager, an executive, an entrepreneur, or the CEO, people just like you get fired for all sorts of reasons, both economically rational and irrational. Many get fired for legal reasons, but not always. Some get fired for doing a bad job. Others get fired because someone didn't like them, even though they were doing a great job. Still others get fired for financial, sexual or other wrongdoing.

Founders aren't immune, not by a long stretch, or any stretch for that matter. Entrepreneurs are regularly forced out, squeezed out and fired from companies they birthed, sometimes to watch painfully from afar as others make millions, while they earn little.

Chief Executive Officers, Chief Financial Officers, Chief Operating Officers, Chief Marketing Officers, and Executive

Vice Presidents of World Wide Sales all regularly get fired. And everyone on down the corporate ladder, including you, can and do get fired and cheated out of money, stock, commissions, and much more.

If you think you're invulnerable, think again.

If you think it can't happen to you, dream on.

Sometimes the person doing the firing even stood up at the employee's, entrepreneur's or executive's wedding. And if you think it's only best men and groomsmen who do the deed, think again. Female employees, executives and entrepreneurs get cheated just like men do. In other words, bridesmaids stab just as badly, but not in as great numbers because women don't yet run corporate America.

The great thing about representing entrepreneurs and founders is they are always on the cutting edge. The cutting edge of their sliver of the world. One is the best in the world of computer chips. If he succeeds, his company will produce transformative chips that allow cars to drive more automatically, tractors to plow more efficiently, and planes to fly more safely. Another is the best when it comes to mobile internet games. The best mobile games are worth billions in revenue, literally.

Executives (who are not entrepreneurs) may not be creating or inventing in the same way, but to represent the finest executives is to learn from the best. One is the best in the world of managing billion-dollar organizations within multi-billion-dollar companies. If she succeeds, her company grows and grows and grows. Another is the best when it comes to running elite sales teams. When he succeeds, his company's stock price goes up and up.

Representing entrepreneurs in Silicon Valley and around the country, I've been blessed with meeting so many on the cutting edge of so many different fields. Medical devices, internet security, computer chips, games, pharmaceuticals, retail, shipping, banking, surgery, software, internet marketing, server farms, finance, the list goes on and on. Constantly surrounded by people who are the best at what they do means learning something new almost every day. It's like an extended college education.

Make no mistake, though. Because entrepreneurs or executives are the best at what they do doesn't mean anything other than that. He may be the best at medical devices, but a terrible friend, father and lover, and crooked to the core. She may be the best at internet security, but the least empathetic, least sympathetic, and biggest liar you have ever met. And it certainly doesn't mean they are good at soccer or swimming or chess or investing or anything other than what their specialty is.

It also doesn't mean the best entrepreneurs and executives know how to negotiate their own employment agreements, nor how to protect themselves in employment, nor the arena of employment negotiations. They may even be failures at company politics.

Just because they got kudos their whole lives at whatever they did, doesn't mean they will survive a layoff or avoid being cheated out of lots of money. I've known multiple CEOs to suffer losses at the hands of fast-talking stockbrokers.

I've spent over twenty-five years giving advice – both legal and business advice – to entrepreneurs, executives, managers and regular employees. But it didn't start out this way, that's for sure.

I went to Princeton University's School of Public and International Affairs. A couple of years after graduating Princeton, I went to Stanford Law School. Like so many who go to Stanford, I stayed in the San Francisco Bay Area, and went to work for the big Palo Alto law firm, Wilson Sonsini Goodrich & Rosati. I did great work, but my assertive style didn't endear me to some. More important, I couldn't stand taking orders from senior attorneys simply because they had been there longer.

Eventually, I hung out my own shingle in Palo Alto. I didn't have enough saved (your basic underfunded business) and almost went under that first year. I'll never forget it. But I had no boss, and no one telling me what to do.

Some great guys over at Wilson Sonsini knew me as a litigator and started referring me litigation work. Eventually, people figured out that if I could litigate a contract, I could probably write one to maximize the chances of avoiding litigation.

All of this metamorphosed into representing entrepreneurs and executives. Basically, many of the big law firms didn't want to represent entrepreneurs and executives personally in their business deals. Why not? Too many conflicts. The big money is made on representing big companies, not individuals.

Most of those early referrers of entrepreneurs and executives cared only about three things: That I did great work, that

I didn't have any conflicts, and that I didn't steal their clients. Check on all accounts.

Eventually I realized there were all these entrepreneurs and executives out there who had no idea how to protect themselves from getting screwed ... and many got screwed.

I decided to run a quarter page add in the *Red Herring*, then Silicon Valley's hot tech magazine, which was low-circulation and, most important, concentrated in Silicon Valley. It was expensive for me just starting out to run a magazine ad, but manageable because I think *Red Herring's* circulation in those days extended from San Francisco in the north to San Jose in the south.

The ad screamed: "Even CEO's Get Fired." One person called to tell me that the grammar was wrong. It should be CEOs, not the possessive CEO's. I ignored that advice.

Before running the ad, I tried it out on a CEO and his wife. The wife – a Stanford MBA – grabbed the ad from me, took a look, rolled her eyes, as if to say, "what an idiot," and dismissingly thrust the ad over to her husband. CEO husband looked at the ad, looked at his wife, looked at me and said, "I would never get caught reading this ad. I'd probably lock myself in a bathroom stall and call you from there."

You would not believe who answered that advertisement. So many were afraid to tell their friends, their colleagues, their associates, their family, they were in trouble jobwise. I was amazed.

My practice grew over time, and by now, I've negotiated or counseled on hundreds and hundreds, if not thousands, of employment and severance agreements. I've negotiated for management teams in M&A transactions, and probably read more stock option, restricted stock and other equity agreements than most venture capitalists.

And I've fought in court and in arbitrations many times when things went wrong. I've represented entrepreneurs, CEOs, CFOs, and EVPs in their legal battles. But I've also represented the delivery driver against the Fortune 100 mothership and multiple non-managerial employees against their private and public employers. At my law firm, we are as comfortable negotiating in the board room as fighting in the court room, although I much prefer building to fighting over spoils.

I have been fortunate over the years to help so many as a lawyer. I'm hoping this book leads me to help (and entertain) you as an author.

I've kept my practice small, to preserve maximum flexibility and because giving entrepreneurs and executives personal advice requires not just an absence of conflicts, it also requires knowing the areas of the law that count, and a certain ability to get along with people, which is hard to find. This is especially true when brutally honest advice is required. I can't tell you how many entrepreneurs' and executives' ideas, suggestions, and expectations I've had to recalibrate over the years.

Brutally honest is the way I practice law. It is also the way I wrote this book. Direct and to the point.

It turns out many an entrepreneur and executive value brutally honest advice, at least when they're paying for the advice. And they often appreciate someone who will say, "no," or "I don't agree with you for the following reasons…," or "I disagree with you and I am going to write you an email to cover my ass because I don't ever want you coming back and complaining that I gave you bad advice."

Who is this book for? You! You, not anyone else but you!

This book is about you the entrepreneur, you the executive, you the manager, you who are just trying to get ahead. You in your employment negotiations with your employer. You in your equity negotiations with whomever. You negotiating your separation agreement. You during the entire lifecycle of your employment relationship.

If you're an entrepreneur or executive, someone with leverage (they need you, they can't do without you, you can always take another job if they don't treat you right) this book will help you learn the lay of the land and figure out what you might demand contractually. How to protect your wages, your equity, your healthcare, or something else you want, need or value.

If you're a regular employee, you'll learn to be aware, to recognize potential employment pitfalls, and how to protect yourself if you're able to do so. You'll also learn that you may have more leverage than you might think, either now or as you advance in your career.

If, on the other hand, you're simply looking for a good read, then this book is for you too! I hope you are entertained by all the "Executive and Entrepreneur Stories" in this book. You can't miss them. They are in their own *sans-serif typeface.*

All of the substantive discussions in the typeface you are looking at right now are factual, as seen through my eyes, anyway. When I discuss how to negotiate a contract, for example, that's non-fiction. In the factual narrative, I describe real-life experiences, anecdotes, negotiating suggestions. The "I" in the substantive discussions is me, this book's author.

But all of the *sans-serif typeface* "Executive and Entrepreneur Stories" in this book are just that, *stories*. They are fictionalized accounts, featuring characters I invented. While the legal issues, situations and circumstances included in this book are based on my years of practicing law, the people, companies, and events that I describe are completely fictitious. No resemblance to any real person or entity is intended or should be inferred.

Even though the Executive and Entrepreneur Stories are pure fiction, they reflect experiences that repeatedly reoccur. I call these "categories of executive and entrepreneurial experiences." For example, one category is: "entrepreneurs and executives stabbed in the back by friends and subordinates." The story in this book featuring a male entrepreneur cut down by his "closest" friend involves invented characters, but the category, the fictionalized experience, repeats itself many times every year in the real world.

"I" in these Executive and Entrepreneur Stories is the first-person fiction. I model the "I" character after myself. In other words, it's the type of language and advice "I" might use or give if I were alive in the fictionalized account I created.

But, I'm *not* alive in the stories, and more important, I'm *not* giving you any legal advice in this book. If you have an issue, you should consult with a lawyer where you live. That's because every situation is different and even though the fact or fiction (or both) in this book might hit home, don't assume your fact pattern "matches" anything you read here. Every circumstance, including yours, is based on its own facts, and no facts, including your facts, are "minor." Which is why you should consult a lawyer in your state for legal advice.

My goal for the Executive and Entrepreneur Stories is to entertain, enliven, and teach. Entertain, via interesting characters. Enliven by transforming a book about employment negotiations into a fast read. Teach by broadening your understanding of themes that repeat again and again in the entrepreneurial-executive world.

You might even find yourself thinking, "hey, that happened to someone I know."

If you wind up thinking, "hey, that happened to me," know you are not alone. The nicest, the shrewdest, the most knowledgeable, the wisest, the smartest, the most capable, really good people, get fired all the time ... for economically rational ... and economically irrational reasons. Protect yourself, if you can. Or at the very least, go forward with your eyes wide open.

2

The Arena

How Much Do They Want You?

"How would I know whether you'll be able to negotiate for seven percent of the company's equity and full accelerated vesting if they terminate you?" I answered honestly.

"But, you're the guy," David insisted. "You've been telling me about this stuff for years. I want to know what you think."

"What I think is: it's all about leverage. If the investors, or Board, or whomever you are going to negotiate with, wants you enough, they'll give you what you want."

"But what I don't know is how much they want you. What I also don't really know is how successful you've been over the years."

"I've told you all the companies I've been with and how well I've done," David asserted.

"Yes, you have ... but on the soccer field. I've never drilled down to really understand. The fact is I don't know all the details of your past successes."

"And with this CEO position you're planning on negotiating for, I certainly need to know more than just your track record to be able to help you. You haven't even told me how much dilution you expect will occur at the company in the next year or two. How could I even begin to figure out whether seven percent is a reasonable ask if I don't know what kind of dilution you expect going forward? Plus, there's lots more information I need to know if you want me to help you."

"Without the details of your particular situation, what I can tell you is that negotiating an employment agreement, or equity agreement, or change in control agreement, or just about any other agreement, is all about leverage. If the investors think you're the only answer and a sure thing for huge returns, they'll stand upside down in the Mississippi River, sing 'God Bless America', and give up the farm for you. But if they think you're just another successful business guy, they'll probably drive a hard bargain."

If You Have It and They Want You, Then You'll Probably Get More

The arena for your entrepreneur or executive negotiation is an immense field of possibilities, open to new ideas, and bounded only by the law and your leverage, or lack thereof.

The venture capitalist investor, the private equity investor, the power player's power player will beg to get in on a potential unicorn, going-through-the-roof, start-up company. He'll give up the store in terms of valuation (taking less percentage of equity in the company), power on the Board, control to the founders, and just about everything else.

On the other hand, the New York private equity investor will screw the founder, CEO, and company brainchild three ways to Sunday, and four ways to every other day, to steal back equity for his private equity fund's limited partners if the founder, CEO, and company brainchild outlives his usefulness.

It doesn't matter whether you are in the computer chip, pharmaceutical, retail, shipping, advertising, internet security, software, professional services, or finance business, if someone wants to hire you to run the show, or someone wants to invest in your enterprise, it's all about leverage. Leverage can take the form of growth prospects, experience, management team quality, expected revenue, anticipated rate of return on either the company or the entrepreneur or executive as manager.

Whatever the substance of the leverage, if you have it and they want you, then you'll command more, if you recognize your value and demand more. Similarly, if you've got the goods in terms of owning a company, and they're desperate to invest, you'll get more capital for less equity than otherwise. That is, if you want to negotiate, or have the stomach to negotiate.

By contrast, when there are limited potential investors, when you're running out of money, in down economies where investment is harder to come by, they may press you for the store before investing. In other words, if they don't want you that badly, and you want them, then you may have to give in, and give in and give in, for your company to survive.

What is your personality? How much are you willing to negotiate? And how much are you willing to risk in your negotiations? You are, after all, a big part of the negotiating arena ... and a player (see next chapter).

Can I get another $25,000 in compensation? Can I negotiate for another point (1%) of equity in the company? I hear these questions all the time. And the answer is: "yes, if you've got the leverage," and "if you have the wherewithal to negotiate."

So much in business is possible, if it's not forbidden by a law or policy. If you can write a term into a contract (that's not illegal), the term can be part of your employment deal or part of the investment you're offering.

America is a gigantic place. The industrialized world, the global world of business is even larger. If you can imagine it, then it can happen ... if you have the leverage to negotiate the deal you're looking for.

He Hates You and He'll Soon Control the Board

"So, what's the problem?" I asked H.L. Cruiser. The message I received said he worked for Mavericks Enterprises.

"Zeus McGregor told me he is going to fire me as soon as Johnnie's off the Board."

"Who is Zeus McGregor, who is Johnnie, and why would he do that?"

"Zeus is Mavericks' CEO, my boss. Johnnie is Johnnie Liu of mobile internet fame. Zeus is going to trade a large tract of land in Montana for Johnnie's Mavericks shares, which means no more Johnnie on the Board."

"The thing is we just bought TWC, Three Ways Camiones," H.L. continued. "It was a $750 million deal, which was really good for the shareholders of both companies, including me."

"What do you do for Mavericks?"

"CTO, Chief Trucking Officer. I run operations. Been doing it for twenty years."

"What does Zeus do?"

"Nothing. Mavericks has a trucking business, by far its biggest business, a rental business, a marketing business, stations, and land. Zeus doesn't know much about anything other than land. He made a ton of money in real estate and thinks he knows everything. In reality, he represents the interests of Maverick's largest shareholder."

"Why is Johnnie Liu doing the land for shares swap when it sounds like Mavericks is doing really well and will be worth much more in the future?"

"Not really sure. Johnnie's super tight lipped, and he's already incredibly wealthy."

"So, what's the Board breakdown?"

"Without Johnnie, two for me, three for Zeus."

"What will happen when you're fired?"

"Many of the trucking team can't stand Zeus. Even the drivers don't like him. They'll leave and go work somewhere else."

"Are you sure, or is that you just overestimating your importance and grandiosely making yourself feel good."

"I hired about 50% of the people who work here. When Mavericks bought TWC, all our key people got sweetheart retention agreements with big payouts. My guess is they'll all wait until their bonuses are paid, and then leave. The thing is, without me and my team, there won't be anyone to keep the trucks moving in any significant way so the value of everyone's shares will plummet after a while."

"Why can't TWC's key employees take over when all the Mavericks' employees are gone?"

"The reason we got the retention agreements and not TWC's employees is because TWC was underperforming so badly on the great routes it had that it was beyond ridiculous."

"Why does Zeus hate you so much?"

"I'm not a 'yes' man. But I think the real problem is I refused to hire his brother, and then told the Board, and the Board said, "No brother."

"So, Zeus would bring the Company down just to fire you? That doesn't make sense. Will the Board let him?"

"Zeus put guys loyal to him on the Board."

"Do Mavericks' other Board members know you're the key to the Company's main source of revenue? The pro-Zeus Board members may love Zeus, but are they going to risk their stakes in the Company to satisfy Zeus' hatreds?"

"They're Zeus' people. They'll probably insist that Zeus hire a replacement for me first. I'm pretty sure that Zeus has been interviewing behind my back."

Sure enough, a month later, Zeus hired a replacement, and after a 3-2 Board vote, Zeus fired H.L. (ostensibly, for not being a team player). As part of his employment contract, H.L. sold his Mavericks shares back to the Company for $36/share.

The employee departures started one day after Mavericks paid its retention bonuses. The brain drain continued for months.

Ten months after the departures began – with sales down, talent drained, and operations a mess – one Board member sold her shares to another Board member for $18/share.

Don't feel too bad for any of Mavericks' Board members. They're all millionaires many times over.

And H.L. started a new enterprise shortly thereafter. Much wiser and battle hardened, H.L.'s new company's corporate documents ensure H.L. will control the company until he no longer wants to do so.

Be Prepared for Economically Irrational Behavior

Boards, bosses, investors, employers – those making the decisions that affect your life and employment – act irrationally all the time. A boss is nothing more than a person with loves, hates, sincerity, blindness, depravity, to mention just a few possible traits. Similarly, Boards or management teams and investor groups are nothing more than an amalgam of individuals with loves, hates, sincerity, blindness, depravity, and a host of other emotions and personality characteristics.

I often hear, "he will …," "she is going to….," "they have to…." settle a case, pay off a claim, concede a term in an employment contract…. And the answer is: "maybe, but maybe not." It depends on the other side's proclivities, perceptions, personality, and thought process, and your ability and willingness to negotiate, demand, implore.

Never underestimate your opponent is an ol' adage from life's playing fields, one that many of us constantly relearn in business. An equally important aphorism: Never underestimate the possibility that "rational actors" will behave irrationally, sometimes insanely irrationally.

But one person's or company's irrationality is sometimes another's shrewdness. Worth remembering.

Take for example, the Executive Vice President, World Wide Sales, who fires the Vice President for the Americas, a world-class salesman, growing revenue year after year and responsible for 75% of the employer's business. If the company's stockholders had a say, they would say "no" to the firing because the value of their shares grows as revenue grows. Thus, the firing of the VP for the Americas is ludicrous from the company's perspective.

But the Executive Vice President's firing of the VP makes total sense from the perspective of an EVP afraid a standout VP will replace him. Firing the league leading VP probably extends the EVP's life expectancy at his employer by many months, if not years. So, the EVP continues to earn a wage, vest his shares – economically rational from his perspective – even while the stockholders suffer. It happens all the time.

The Dynamo and the Chief Financial Officer

A workaholic dynamo, Linda has an astonishing brain for managing health care businesses. She has what they call in grad school, "superior business acumen." Only the highest grades in high school, in college and in business school. At her public employer, Linda was the youngest person ever to make executive vice president. She made millions in stock options and restricted stock.

After eleven years, Linda left her lucrative career to join a private equity-backed turnaround in her hometown as its Chief Operating Officer.

The CEO and PE investors of the new company assured Linda that she would become CEO in a few years, and in six to seven years, if the economy remained strong, she would be very rich.

The new company's Board, an extension of the PEs who purchased the company, granted Linda four percent of the company's fully diluted equity, with vesting triggered by performance metrics linked to revenue and market share. Linda trusted the PEs – her equity sat unprotected.

The best part about the transition – Linda returned home. Nothing compared to Lake Michigan, Wrigley, and Soldier Field (even remodeled), and perhaps, Linda's favorite, the iconic Chicago dog.

Years one, two and three were a successful blur. Linda labored late into the night, night after night, taking only eight days of vacation. She travelled everywhere. Linda even earned a quick vest of her first equity tranche when the company's performance triggered the vesting metric a year earlier than expected.

On the personal front, all systems were go. Linda and her husband bought a great house; twins arrived; Linda's husband got a nice promotion; the couple found a great nanny.

Just shy of Linda's third anniversary, the couple bought one of those yacht-like boats the wealthy keep in Burnham Harbor between the stadium and old Meigs Field. Linda and her husband, who already had an outsized mortgage on their home, took a big loan out on the boat because Linda's prospects were so strong.

Linda dropped by her boss' office one day. Strangely, HR was in the room.

The boss opened: "Things aren't working out with you and our company. You don't have a long-term career here. It's time for you to find another job...."

Unadulteratedly shocked, completely blindsided, Linda traversed a hazy daze for weeks. She just did not understand – things had seemed to be going so well. She was supposed to be the CEO soon.

Anger at the treatment followed.

Also, not good, one morning on the fuel dock, a drunken idiot plowed his yacht into Linda's, and both insurance carriers refused to pay.

Unbeknownst to Linda, her days were at risk from the start. At least that's what an experienced observer would have told her.

The problem for Linda – The company's CFO wanted the CEO job. And the CFO was no newbie. His resume was a long one. His successes included serving as CFO and COO at three turnarounds, a private company that sold for north of $2 billion, and a public company whose stock doubled during his tenure.

The CFO had joined the company also expecting to be CEO. At the end of the day, the-less-than-honest PEs opted for the CFO.

The CFO wanted Linda gone, probably to eliminate the threat, and convinced the PEs to let her go.

There was no one to save Linda. A problem no number of successes, no number of late nights, could counteract.

The PEs were jerks on exit. Ignoring Linda's many requests, they refused to accelerate the vesting of any equity, and instead, to Linda's dismay, repurchased Linda's stock – as their contracts allowed – at a low value they essentially determined.

Ultimately Linda got another job and the drunken idiot's insurance carrier finally paid. But only after many months of stress.

Linda swears she'll never again join a company without protecting her equity.

You Need Protection

You wouldn't buy a house without purchasing insurance, would you? You wouldn't drive a car around without insurance, would you? Why then, if you can – and sometimes you can't – would you join a company without protecting yourself and your family?

What are you protecting against? You're protecting against being put out on the street by your employer with nothing but your final paycheck.

In most at-will states, your employer can fire you whenever it wants to do so (assuming you're not an academic with tenure, in a union under a collective bargaining contract, or in some other special circumstance). And it doesn't matter whether you're the CEO or the receptionist. Your employer can show you the proverbial door for any reason at all, or no reason (though not for an illegal reason, such as you're too old or the wrong race).

Protecting yourself in the employment arena often means getting money, company-paid benefits, vesting of options, delivery of stock or possibly other benefits from your employer *on or after* the day you're fired, laid off, or quit for mistreatment.

As one example, the currency (possibly your currency) for oversized gains in employment is often equity. Equity is the stock or stock options that founders, employees and executives have, or will have, in their companies. It could be options to purchase stock in that private start-up that everyone hopes will go public at multiples and multiples. Or it could be lots of stock (or restricted stock) in the mature public company that you hope goes up and up.

However, if you're an "at-will" employee, you could lose all your equity if you're fired before it vests or is delivered to you. And while there are folks out there as honest as the day is long, and while you may not be stabbed in the back by those who stood up at your wedding, there are a lot of people in business – not just vulture capitalists, hateful CEOs, and I'd-drive-my-car-over-my-grandma-to-increase-my-LPs-stake-by-a-penny-a-share private equity guys – who will do you in for all sorts of reasons. That's why you protect yourself and your family. Protection, in this example, means holding on to some or all of your equity if your employer fires you and walks you to the door.

It's more than bad characters you have to worry about. Job interviewers paint overly rosy pictures. Bosses change. People move on. Employers grow exponentially. Companies get purchased. Businesses downsize.

In other words, the company you hire into, may not be the employer you join on day one, or may not be the same place down the road. And the fantastic boss you once had – or if you are a CEO, the great Board members you once cherished – may not be the same boss or Board members later, and those remaining may not want you for any number of reasons.

One of the ways to protect yourself that I write more about in future chapters is the professional prenuptial agreement, which is a well-written offer letter or employment agreement that doubles as a severance agreement. If you have one and your employer fires you without cause, then you can probably stick out your hand and say something like: "I think your decision to can me is dumb, but just pay me what you owe me and vest me as agreed – see ya." Securing a strong professional prenuptial agreement in the negotiating arena is like scoring a touchdown, hitting a grand slam, or netting a hat trick.

There are also other ways to protect yourself in the negotiating arena which I discuss in later chapters. One example is the back-end separation agreement (benefits negotiated for at the end of employment). Another is the change in control agreement (benefits paid on a corporate change in control).

Unfortunately, most lower level employees don't have the leverage to negotiate for a professional prenuptial or other type of protective agreement. In fact, some companies refuse to offer protection of any type to those other than the CEO and maybe CFO.

But the truth is also that you may have more leverage than you think, this being a big America. Imagine adding a simple one liner into your offer letter – "if you fire me without cause, you will pay me ... [vest me ....]"

Think About What Drives Your Employer

When you're negotiating your employment agreement or separation agreement, or any other employment-based agreement for that matter, think about what drives the other side (your would-be or ex-employer). See if you can use those motivations to your advantage as you negotiate to maximize your return – best employment agreement, best separation agreement, etc.

Most employers want to control their employees, from CEO on down. But there are many factors that drive employers, especially because there are myriad employers out there. For example, some employers are stimulated by a desire to foster a warm, collegial atmosphere. Others, however, believe they shine best when their employees compete with each other.

Employers are often smart about the employment arena where they play. New coders just out of university in Silicon Valley, California, for example, might score huge signing bonuses, great pay and excellent equity. Why? Because their employers are desperate for the best coders. But even in this scenario, that signing bonus probably must be repaid if the newbie leaves his or her employment in the first year or two.

On the flip side, diverse considerations motivate employers to offer separation agreements even though they are not obligated to do so by law. Some feel it is the right thing to do. Others fear a lawsuit (and want that release!). Still others desire to offer a sense of security to their at-will employees in case the business someday says to them: "sayonara."

Many companies have policies and plans that memorialize "who they are and what they provide" to their employees. Some of these policies or plans may provide for pay or other benefits to those who are fired. Check out your potential employer's policies and plans before you sign up to work for it, or better yet, before starting to negotiate the terms of your employment (no reason to negotiate for something you're probably going to receive anyway under an existing policy).

The Shifting Arena

Although laden with immense possibilities, the entrepreneurial and executive negotiating arena shifts as discussions progress. Figuring out where you are in the "life cycle" of your entrepreneur and executive negotiation might help you land a better deal. How hard to push, when to make a stand, when to concede are often important considerations.

For example, "take a hike" at the beginning of a negotiation may not be "take a hike" at the end of the negotiation. Sparring entrepreneurs and executives and their would-be employers often say all sorts of things at the outset. However, "take a hike" after five iterations of an employment agreement may be where the line in the sand is drawn.

Practically speaking, at all but the highest levels, the life cycle of a negotiation may be a take-it-or-leave-it employment offer letter. Entrepreneurs and executives with leverage and regular people like you and me with leverage, however, often spar in real employment and equity negotiations.

The ability to determine where you are in a negotiation is often something you (and others) learn by experience. Thus, during your negotiation, you might want to consult someone who has done it before, or many times before. You might find her very useful as you negotiate.

You might also want someone with experience to help you think objectively during your negotiations. No matter how much of a star you are, it's very hard to be objective when it's your livelihood, your money, your stock, on the line. The lawyer's way of expressing this is: A lawyer who represents himself has a fool for a client. An older adage with the same message: A person in the metaphorical jail cannot help himself. A wise advisor can help you see the entire negotiating arena.

Things to Remember:

- If you have it and they want you, then you'll probably get more.
- What you are able to negotiate depends on your leverage (and your willingness to use it).
- Leverage takes many forms – figure out how much leverage you have.
- Be prepared for economically irrational behavior.
- You need protection.
- Many things drive your employer – use them to your advantage, if possible.
- Your negotiating arena will shift as things progress – figuring out where you are in the life cycle of your negotiation might help you negotiate a better contract.

3

Entrepreneurs, Executives, Founders & Company Decisionmakers

Maybe I'll Clean House?

"Thanks so much for meeting me here," John Aput said to Deluge Reponer who had just appeared at Mangos & Machos Bar, a local watering hole. M&M served Caipirinhas, John's favorite drink.

John is a long-time venture capitalist with Blarney Hedgehog Ventures. Blarney's main offices are over on Sand Hill Road.

"What's up?" Deluge asked. Deluge oozed experience and success. Deluge has been a CEO, a COO, and even once an EVP of World Wide Sales, although he doesn't really like sales. Most recently, Deluge ran an internet security company that he sold after only three years at the helm.

Deluge and John were on a number of Boards together. They also have five or six mutual friends.

"I'm looking for a CEO to replace the founder of one of my portfolio companies, Z5999 Finaplode," John explained. "Z5999 has a suite of great financial products.

Its revenues are in the $4-5-million-year range and the market is huge."

"I have no experience in the financial space," Deluge replied. "But as you've heard me say many times, a good manager can manage any corporation, no matter what it does and no matter whether it's for profit or non-profit."

"Why are you getting rid of the founder, who I'm guessing is also the CEO?" Deluge asked.

"The founder is a genius," John replied. "He is creative. He fixes problems others don't even see. And he codes better than anyone at the Company. But he can't manage people. He's not the right person to bring this company to the next stage. And given his personality, there's no way to keep him on at the company with a new CEO on board."

"How many employees does Z5999 have?" Deluge asked.

"45 now, but the Company is going to scale. We hope to have 70 on board by the end of the year, and to hire another 100 to 200 here and in Europe next year. I know you've scaled companies before, which is why I thought we should talk," John said.

"Are any of the employees loyal to the founder, and are there any others who need to go?"

"The engineering team is solid. Maybe we'll lose one or two, but they'll mostly stay put. The stock they're vesting has a big upside if the company can scale." John answered.

"The management team respects the founder's genius, but don't like his management style. The team will stay if you want them. But if you take the job, you can bring in whoever you want. Most of the top execs are start-up types who don't have experience scaling the way we're planning to scale the company."

"Wouldn't be the first place I had to clean house, so that's not a problem," Deluge replied. "All start-ups need real people to manage them at some point."

"I brought this slide deck along to show you, so you can get a feel for what we're talking about," John said as he handed Deluge a glossy presentation.

Entrepreneurs and Executives

Entrepreneurs and executives are not the same thing. They can be. But not necessarily. The skill sets are very different. The entrepreneur and executive, even the entrepreneur-executive are often light years apart.

Are you ready to spend hours creating a company with the real possibility your enterprise will go belly up? Are you ready to invest money and hours and hours of time, keep those flickering bulbs burning, and endure the stress, all in the hopes of making a bigger, better enterprise, building a superior widget, process or service, securing your future, and perhaps the futures of employees, investors, and family members? If you are, then you are probably an entrepreneur, or at least have the entrepreneurial light in you.

Entrepreneurs come in all sizes and sorts, from Maine to Georgia, Washington to California, and from around the world. Entrepreneurs start and build all kinds of companies.

Somewhere, sometime, there were entrepreneurs forming and building cement factories, tire plants, coat hanger businesses, chemical companies, farming businesses. Wait … they're still building those companies!

And let's not forget about the chocolate entrepreneurs, ice cream entrepreneurs, retail entrepreneurs, building today, yesterday, and tomorrow.

Most businesses in America are small enterprises. How do you think they got started? Entrepreneurs.

But, these days, headlines tend to focus on a select group of entrepreneurial start-ups, like those in the internet security, software, social media, chip design, biotech, finance, pharmaceutical, medical devices, and autonomous driving space.

While entrepreneurs populate mom and pop shops and other businesses around the country, the type of entrepreneurs I discuss in this book are those who attempt to start and build large new companies quickly, often hoping for an exit in one to ten years. An exit like a big sale or going public.

Some of these entrepreneurs may self-finance, particularly if the founder has had prior success. Many, however, seek external funding from friends and family, angel investors, venture capitalists, private equity investors, debt financiers or strategic investors. They give up percentages of their babies every time they accept capital. And they often need protection from the world around them.

The world around them may include the executive world.

Do you run companies? Do you manage? Do you direct? Do you have an MBA, grad schooling? Or do you manage intuitively, perhaps, learned how to run a business in the school of hard knocks? If so, then you are probably an executive, would-be executive, or at least executive material.

Executives usually manage people and know about organizational behavior and frequently about systems, such as a finance system, an accounting system, a sales system, a human resources system. Sometimes they create and design, but not necessarily. And they don't often scrape by just to keep the lights on, in the way a founder does anyway.

Executives manage myriad companies, of all sizes and in all industries. Some are great at managing $5 million-a-year operations, but terrible at running $500 million-a-year enterprises, and vice versa.

Executives run public companies. Executives manage private companies. And some of those private companies are larger than most public companies. Just look at Mars or Fidelity. Or the real estate empires fueling multiple NFL owners.

Whatever they're managing, executives, like entrepreneurs, often need protection from the world around them, especially from a firing, whether they see it coming or not.

Just because you're a top-notch executive, doesn't mean you'll be a good entrepreneur, although you might be. You may very well may be creative in directing the organizations you manage, but that doesn't necessarily mean you can start a successful company. Executives often depend on others to do the inventing, to suffer the "we-might-not-make-it" life cycles of the business.

On the flip side, you could be a fantastic entrepreneur, a serial founder, successfully founding company after company. But that doesn't mean you get along with people or are able to manage them. Nor does it mean you can competently run the company you just founded. Being the best entrepreneur may lead to being a stellar executive. But not necessarily.

Both Ends of the Spectrum

"I have no choice. I have to sell," Larissa exclaimed.

"Why?"

"Because my investor insists on a quick return," Larissa responded. "And he controls the cash flow. We tried to raise another financing round six months ago, but the investor kept 'pooh-poohing' the term sheets that came in and we're out of money now."

"So, what are the terms of the sale?"

"$50 million all cash. It's a fast close – the deal is supposed to close in a month."

"How will the $50 million be distributed?"

"The preferences on the Series A and Series B Preferred Stock are only $10 million, so the preferred converts to Common Stock one-to-one. The investors own 50% of the Company, I own 40% and the employees own 10% fully diluted."

"So, the investors take $25 million, you gross $20 million and the employees take $5 million. That's the 50%-40%-10% stock breakdown. Or is there debt that must be paid off first?"

"Our balance sheet is clean. We don't have any debt. But the employees are still vesting their options and the term sheet is all cash. The employees together are 50% vested, some more, some less. The acquirer is not assuming or substituting for the employees' options so all the employees' options will be cancelled. Instead, the acquirer is going to offer a retention bonus pool to keep the employees it wants to keep."

"Are you going to accelerate the vesting of the employees' options, so they are fully vested at the close?"

"Our company's equity plan says the options for unvested shares can be cancelled in an acquisition if the acquirer does not assume or substitute for the employees' options."

"OK. But is your Board going to accelerate the vesting of your employees' options, so the employees receive the full benefit of their hard work?"

"No. That's not what the plan requires."

"So, what you are telling me, if I have the math right, is that when the employees' options for unvested shares are wiped out at the close, you will own 42% of the Company and take home $21 million, not $20 million, the investors will own 52.5% of the Company and receive $26.25 million, not $25 million, and the employees will own only 5.5% of the Company, down from 10% with full vesting, and take home only $2.75 million, instead of $5 million with the full vesting."

"Sounds right."

"So how can I help you?"

"The acquirer wants to subject 50% of my $21 million to vesting over two years, and I need help protecting myself in case the acquirer fires me before I get my $10.5 million."

"Don't you think the employees deserve to have their options fully accelerated? They helped you build your company so you could make $20 million in less than four years. Do you really think the employees understood that the company's equity plan wiped out their options if an acquisition happened?"

"No one negotiated for any acceleration in a change in control."

Founders – Abusees and Abusers

Founders sometimes get royally ripped off in entrepreneurial America. On the other hand, founders sometimes cheat others unbelievably badly.

You the founder may need protection. But, you the co-founder, executive, or regular employee may need protection from your company's founder.

Founders birth start-ups, and after that, they desperately attempt to nurture their enterprises through infancy, and then beyond.

It's the founder's dreams, his or her drive, stick-to-itiveness, and risk-taking that illuminates the entrepreneurial path. Founders are often creators and inventors, but they need not be. Occasionally it is an MBA, manager or financier who starts the company, sometimes in concert with creative or technological leaders.

Abusive founders fire arrogantly, act whimsically, scream tyrannically, cheat you and others out of equity and commissions. Their wrath can reign indiscriminately ... on colleagues, subordinates, managers, investors. Some abuse seemingly because they have the ability, the power to do so. In other words, founders have been known to screw you and everyone around them. Victims just like you sometimes feel devastatingly mistreated, wronged beyond belief, even shellshocked.

Note that abusing subordinates and making underlings rich are distinct phenomena. Oppressive founders have made tens of millions for those like you who survived their organizations. Your boss may be a hold-the-phone-away screamer, but you and others who survive may also get rich off his spoils.

However, founders have also caused many a needless bankruptcy. The start-up world is inundated with failures driven into the ground by founders who stayed too long on the job. Some of these founders were abusers, others myopic, and still others simply naïve.

On the other hand, founders have suffered monumental abuse. Legions of founders have been forced out of companies they birthed, their equity squeezed out (recapped), forced to watch as others bring their baby public. Founders have lost out at the hands of fellow founders, colleagues, investors, venture capitalists, private equity principals, lawyers, friends who stood up at their wedding, the list is long.

Startups where multiple founders share equity and power equally are disasters in the making. Founder fights and founders forcing out founders are not a guarantee. But if I went to Vegas, I would give odds that a founder fight will happen at some point.

Just because founders know each other, are college buddies, travelled together or worked together for years, does not mean they will play well together in business. It also does not mean they will treat each other honestly, caringly, or in a humane manner. What is certain, however, is that founder vs. founder squeeze outs happen all the time.

Shrewd investors know this. Sometimes they seek to divide and conquer, ganging up with one or more founders against a fellow founder. Remember that if the forced-out founder's stock is not fully vested, it may be forfeited, to the investors and remaining founders' potential profit. Squeezed out founders litter the start-up world.

Take, for example, a three-founder start-up, where the founders divide the company's stock equally, where their unprotected equity (restricted stock subject to repurchase) vests pro-rata over four years with a 25% cliff vest at one year assuming continuing employment, where each serve on the start-up's three-person Board, and where one founder serves as CEO, the second as CTO and the third as EVP of Engineering.

If six months into the startup, the CTO and EVP decide to fire the CEO, they can do so, two votes to one. Since no shares have yet vested (because of the 25% one-year cliff vest), the departing founder loses all of his equity. In the absence of special contracting or voting rights agreements, it is often all about who controls the board of directors and how that Board is elected.

What happens to the lost equity? It is redistributed back to the founders. Not directly. But that's the way the math works. After the company repurchases the fired CEO's stock, the departing founder owns 0% of the start-up, whereas each surviving founder now owns 50% of the start-up's equity.

Why would two founders gang up on a third? Innumerable reasons, legitimate and illegitimate.

Sometimes, founder firings make real business sense, especially when a founder is destroying the business he created. Other founder firings, however, result from misfeasance. Still others are driven by malicious malfeasance.

They Give Us Jobs

Employers provide us with jobs.

Your employer may be small, medium-size, large or a gigantic multinational. It may be for profit, or a non-profit, private or public. Your employer may be organized as a C-Corp., a Subchapter S-Corp., a limited liability company or in some other way. It may be headquartered in Alaska, Arizona, Maine, Michigan or another place. Your employer may make almost everything, or nothing at all.

Your employer may be one of so many types. However, in terms of employers, I concentrate here on entrepreneur-driven enterprises, private employers of all sizes large enough to have managers, and publicly traded employers.

The Ultimate Authority

The board of directors (aka, the "Board") is the ultimate authority in an American corporation. The Board usually does not run things day-to-day. Nor do individual Board members, unless they are executives (for example, the CEO often sits on her employer's Board) or there is an "executive chairman" (meaning the Board chairman has a day-to-day oversight role of some type). Boards are responsible for big-picture strategic matters, for ensuring that management does its job, and for setting management compensation.

Boards hire CEOs. Thus, you, the soon-to-be hired CEO, negotiate with the Board (or a Board representative) of your would-be employer. And it is against the proclivities of Boards that CEOs require protection. Because Boards fire CEOs just as they hire them.

Large Boards and Boards of publicly traded companies (meaning, their stock trades on the public markets) often create committees to take responsibility over certain key areas. For example, a Board may appoint a compensation committee to oversee your executive compensation and an audit committee to oversee your company's accounting and financial life. In some cases, certain committees are required by the stock exchanges on which their companies publicly trade.

Public company Boards and compensation committees often must follow rules, rules promulgated by Congress, the United States Securities and Exchange Commission (SEC), the accounting authorities, and others. Disclosure is critical, and Boards and compensation committees are often constrained by parties representing various corporate interests.

Private companies are another animal. Many of their Boards and compensation committees, if they have ones, can often do what they want, or if not exactly what they want, have freer reign. At start-up companies with outside investors, the investors frequently make the decisions about management compensation.

Senior Executives

CEO, Chief Financial Officer ("CFO"), Chief Operating Officer ("COO"), Chief Revenue Officer ("CRO"), Chief Technology Officer ("CTO"), Chief Medical Officer ("CMO"), Chief Marketing Officer (also "CMO"), President, Executive Vice President of World Wide Sales ... these are some of the titles of a company's most senior management, sometimes called "C-Suite Executives." They typically report to or are on the team of the CEO. They set company policy and run the day-to-day operations of your employer.

If you'll be on the CEO's team, the CEO will probably be the ultimate decisionmaker in your hiring, although your company's by-laws may make certain positions, for example, the CFO, officers of the Board. This generally means that the Board must officially vote to hire and fire these officers, but a Board will usually not do so without the CEO's backing.

The CEO and management team are in charge of hiring their employer's most senior managers. If you're being hired for a senior position, then someone on the CEO's staff will probably be the officer tasked with hiring you.

Headhunters

You can hire a headhunter who will be loyal to you, who you pay, and who may look out for your best interests. It does happen.

More often, however, headhunters are hired for a "retained search" by an employer seeking to fill a position. For example, a company's Board or EVP of Human Resources (HR) might retain a headhunter to find the company's new Chief Marketing Officer. The headhunter then attempts to locate talent (that's you) to fill the position. Generally, headhunters send their clients (the companies that hired them!) a list of qualified candidates for the employers to consider.

Note that headhunters often refer to themselves as executive search specialists or something similar. And they usually call the places they work, "executive search firms."

Headhunters are paid in different ways. A popular approach is to pay the headhunter a percentage (e.g., 50%) of the executive's first year salary. Other times, headhunters are paid a fixed fee.

Unless you've retained your own headhunter, you're not the headhunter's client. The employer is. The employer does the paying and the loyalty runs to the employer.

And that headhunter may not earn a dime until you sign up to work for the employer. In other words, if you don't sign on the dotted line, no cash flows into the headhunter's bank account. Getting the idea?

Headhunters often don't call in lawyers to assist their executives (even though executives could sometimes use the assistance). Why? Would you want to insert someone into a deal that might interrupt the path between your paycheck and you?

Comp Consultants

Companies hire all sorts of consultants and contractors. In the employment world, especially in the public company and large private enterprise executive hiring world, compensation (comp) consultants are one of the most important (after headhunters). They're often hired by Board compensation committees.

Comp consultants are supposed experts on what you should earn. They advise on how much salary, bonus, commission, equity and other benefits you should receive. There's no real secret to what comp consultants do. They research and compile data to figure out what people are paid.

Charts appear to be the purview of the comp consultants. Their charts often purport to show various compensation structures for your potential job. Typically, they contain three important bands. The comp band across the chart showing the 75th percentile of comp for the job you want, the 50th percentile and the 25th percentile.

What compensation band the comp committee or Board is willing to settle on depends on many factors. Ultimately, though it's mostly an expression of leverage – how badly your prospective employer wants you compared to how badly you want to work for your potential employer and how hard you're willing to push in the negotiations. You, the soon-to-be-hired executive, might want to argue that your pay should be in the

95th to 99th percentile because, of course, you are the best. Doesn't that make sense?

Your Employer's Lawyers

Your employer or prospective employer probably has one or more lawyers, maybe in-house, maybe outside counsel, or maybe it has both. Those attorneys' job is to enthusiastically advocate for your employer, not for you.

This may really upset you, especially if you just got fired, are attempting to negotiate a separation agreement, and the employer's counsel says, "no." Or, if your ex-employer instructs the attorney to go after you. You might even have once counted the now-hostile corporate lawyer as a friend. While you might not like what's going on, you should be ready for it.

As a general matter, you should always be cautious about what you tell your employer's lawyer, and even what you tell your non-lawyer co-worker. Your co-worker may be more of a colleague, or perhaps back-stabber, than a friend, and in any event, your co-worker may have obligations as an employee to tell your employer what you said. Less nefariously, your co-worker might be well intended, just oblivious to the consequences of repeating what you told him.

But you should be super wary of telling your employer's lawyer anything other than what's required. Because no matter how tight you think you may be with your corporate-attorney-friend, no matter how good a "friend" that lawyer might appear to be, no matter even the romance you may have had, your corporate-attorney-friend is *duty bound* to advocate for his client, which is your employer, not you. And if that means reporting something you told him in confidence, so be it.

Strategics and Venture Capitalists

"We need to raise $10 million this round to get us through the next 18 months," V.F. Prunedanish, CEO of Big D Devices, "BDD" for short, confided.

"KVP," Prunedanish continued, "has agreed to lead the round, but they are asking for a 2.5X liquidation preference, and I think that's too much."

"Kissme Venture Partners?"

"Yes."

"You mean KVP wants a guaranteed return of two-and-a-half times their investment before the common stockholders take anything from a BDD sale?"

"Yes."

"What's the valuation they are proposing?"

"$80 million pre-money."

"Is that good?

"Not bad," said Prunedanish. "And J.P. Enterprises said it will invest $4 million."

"Who?"

"A strategic investor. They own a suite of medical devices, but have lost millions on their R&D programs in the last four or five years. Investing in us is cheaper than doing their own R&D," Prunedanish explained.

"What's J.P. Enterprises' goal?"

"If we succeed, they'll probably buy us," Prunedanish replied. "They're public and have a boatload of cash. They could easily quadruple our revenue in six to nine months just selling through their distribution network. It's unbelievable."

"Can you get another strategic to invest?"

"Maybe."

"Strategics probably won't bother you and will let you run BDD the way you want to run it. That's because their focus is usually elsewhere, like someday buying you. It's sometimes much better having a strategic who lets you run your company the way you want to run it, than having meddling VCs on your Board who can be a real pain, no matter how famous they are."

"On the other hand, strategics do have their downsides. Strategics looking to buy you will sometimes do their best to keep your sales price down so they can pay as little as possible. VCs, however, almost always want to sell at top dollar because that returns more money to their funds and LPs."

"A top tier VC can really help us, I think," said Prunedanish.

"Help you do what? If you can get two or three strategics to take $8 or $9 million of the round, and keep the terms of the investment favorable to BDD, you have 18 months of runway. You might not need to raise after that. BDD is going to succeed or fail based on its products."

"Kissme is known to have some partners who really meddle. They've fired CEOs doing a good job. Is it worth it just to get a top tier VC?

"What kind of preference does J.P. Enterprises want?"

"1X."

"1X compared to KVP's 2.5X. That's a big difference."

"1X is a lot better, that's for sure."

Your Employer's Investors

If you're a founder or CEO, it's a good idea to know who your investors are, and as best as you can, learn what drives them and how they are prone to act and react. Investors – whether in public companies or private companies – can be incredibly supportive, extraordinarily destructive, completely hands on, or totally hands off. It all depends on the investor, situation and context.

An institutional investor at a public company is a company, organization, money manager or fund that specializes in investing in public companies. Institutional investors include pension funds, banks, insurance companies, mutual funds and endowments. Fidelity, Vanguard and CalPERS are examples of institutional investors.

If you're going into a big publicly traded company, the company's institutional investors probably won't express any direct opinion, one way or the other, on your hiring.

However, their views may constrain what your would-be employer offers you in compensation and benefits. On certain big-ticket, or hot-button executive compensation issues, institutional investors may pressure the Board, especially if the institutional investors have guidelines for pay practices. The institutional investors also often have advisors (institutional advisors) which themselves may have policies and opinions that constrain the Board, especially if the Board calculates its institutional investors will adopt the policies and opinions of their advisors.

In addition, your negotiating stance with your public employer may be constrained by the prior, or prospective, votes of institutional and other shareholders in your prospective public employer's required "say on pay" vote, a non-binding vote the shareholders take on the CEO's compensation package at least once every three years. This is because, even though it's a non-binding vote, your Board or would-be Board probably doesn't want your pay package to be voted down by the shareholders.

Don't confuse public companies' institutional investors with private company investors. They may be the same. But usually not.

Self-funded founders, angel investor groups, high net worth individuals, venture capitalists, private equity players, and debt financiers are some of those who fund private companies. "Strategic investors" (e.g., a joint venture partner, potential acquirer, or potential customer doubling as an investor) also provide capital. Some of these investors may sit on the private company's Board.

There are so many types of private investors that there is no private funder archetype across private entities. Investors vary like people. Investor funds vary as well – they're nothing more than one or more individuals making decisions for them.

Some private company investors will give you everything you ask for and leave you alone. Others will fire you on a dime, and then do everything to steal back your equity. Some will insist they can do a better job than you, even if they have never run a company before. You must know who the investors are and what they (metaphorically, in the case of entities) think to understand with whom and with what you are dealing.

Investors and their managers – in both private and public companies – may have personal or institutional interests that trump your best interests or the best interests of management, your employer, or the stockholders as a whole.

Always remember that the investor's job is to make money for that investor (if she's an angel investor, or an institution investing for the institution), the investor's investors (if the investor manages a fund), or whomever the investor is responsible for. Those interests may not be aligned with yours. For example, you may hope to build the company you founded into a juggernaut, the leading player in the market, whereas, two of your key investors may be looking for a fast sale of the company, one because she wants quick liquidity to purchase the ski retreat she always wanted, and the second because she wants to report strong returns to the limited partners of the fund she manages.

Things to Remember:

- Consider whether you are an entrepreneur or executive or both.
- Founders can badly abuse you. And founders can be badly abused. You may need protection from the founder of your company. And the founder of your company may need protection from others.
- Know your employer; Know who's hiring you.
- If you're a CEO (or perhaps other C-Suite officer), make sure you know your Board. Boards hire and fire CEOs.
- Headhunters may land you the job, but they're usually paid by, and loyal to, your employer.
- Your employer's lawyer is duty bound to advocate for your employer, not you.
- Investors can sometimes play a role in your executive employment world, especially if you're a founder or CEO.

4

You and Your Advisors

Can I Refer My CEO to You?

"Hi, I'm Eugenia Armstrong. I'm General Counsel of Folded Leg Associates, FLA for short. Can I refer my CEO Will Pinot over to you?"

"Nice to meet you Eugenia, by telephone, anyway. Sure, what's up?"

"Will has been doing a great job. Our company has been growing for the past nine quarters. Our revenues are good. But, for some reason the Board wants to make a change."

"What's going on?"

"The lead Board member thinks he can do a better job running the company."

"Does he have experience?"

"No. It doesn't make any sense to me. But I told Will that I can't advise him on anything and that he should go see you."

"Not the first time. A lawyer I know referred me a CEO a couple of years ago. Then the lawyer negotiated the separation agreement opposite me. When it was over, the lead investor took over as CEO. First thing he did was fire the lawyer because the investor-CEO said he gave away too much in the exit negotiations."

You and Whoever's Across the Table

Reflect on who you are and your personality. Before founding a company, accepting funding, or beginning your job search, consider who you're best suited to work for or with, which job or jobs best reflect your personality, where and with whom you'd like to work, and other factors important to you and your decision making.

And don't forgot about the person across the table. Reflect! Ask yourself: Do I really want to work for him and his organization? Should I accept money from her or her company?

Of course, your disposition and the dispositions of all the other players in your entrepreneurial and executive employment arena matter!

Some of us are great negotiators. Others of us can't negotiate our way out of a box.

Some of us are as honest as the day is long. Others of us will lie, cheat and steal to get what we want.

Some of us are great to work for. Others of us are nightmares to toil under.

Some of us are arrogant beyond belief. Others of us are as humble as the proverbial pie.

Some of us are the best at what we do. Other of us are pretenders. Still others of us prove the Peter Principal.

Getting the idea? Consider everything before advancing forward.

It's Not Your Company Any More

Nate, a brilliant software designer, loved his Colorado weed. It appeared to infuse him, free him, enable him to write ever better software updates. Nate was a repeat success in the software world, responsible for billions in revenue.

And Protect-U, Nate's start-up, was a success. Revenues had doubled in the past year. Protect-U had 30 full time employees in Colorado, six others scattered around the United States and another 20 contractors in India.

Fundraising had come easy to Nate. Protect-U raised $25 million in three rounds of financing (an A, B and C round), each time with a higher valuation and a new lead investor to price the round. Protect-U's most recent valuation, at the C-round, was $175 million pre-money (the company's value before the C-round investment).

Representatives from each of the lead investors, the former CEO of a public company, and Nate served on Protect-U's five-person board of directors. The investors owned 65% of Protect-U's fully diluted capital. Nate owned 21% and employees and others owned 14%, in the aggregate.

After about six months on Protect-U's Board, Protect-U's Series C lead investor Curtis Glucker decided

Protect-U's growth trajectory would be much more rapid if Protect-U replaced Nate with a dynamic, well groomed, repeat CEO working with his fund's incubator.

Unbeknownst to Nate, after a series of late-night phone calls during the first week of June, Curtis convinced the other two investor Board members that Nate must be replaced.

The second Saturday in June, Nate received a text from Curtis asking to speak. Nate was designing Protect-U's next software release when the text came in. Forty-five minutes later, Curtis delivered the message: It was time for Nate to leave Protect-U, but the Company wanted to treat him well. Curtis offered Nate 12 months of severance pay and paid COBRA premiums. Nate could stay on Protect-U's Board, Curtis said, if Nate did not disrupt.

Nate was devastated. Protect-U had been his heart and soul for the past six years. 18-hour days (including ganja-aided software-design extravaganzas), day-after-day-after-day, week-after-week-after-week, year-after-year, with nary a holiday.

Nate explained to Curtis that Protect-U's continued growth depended on him, that things were going well. Curtis was unmoved.

Eventually, Nate stooped to begging to continue at Protect-U.

"Not happening," Curtis explained.

Nate did not have the Board votes to keep his job. And he did not have sufficient Protect-U stock to replace any of the Board members. Nate had lost control of his company.

There was nothing Nate could do, but seek a better exit package.

Nate didn't own any of the software he had designed either. When Nate incorporated Protect-U, he assigned all of his Protect-U-related intellectual property to the Company. Thereafter, he had signed a proprietary information and inventions agreement confirming that all post-incorporation work belonged to Protect-U.

Two weeks later, the parties inked a formal separation agreement.

Nate sat at home, very much alone.

Do You Need Help?

If you would like or need assistance, then seek help. You might want help negotiating a protective prenuptial employment agreement. You might want someone to explain to you the ins and outs of your company's corporate governance documents. Perhaps, you would like strategic advice vis-à-vis a back-end separation ask. Whatever area in the entrepreneurial and executive world you need advice in, there are lots of people who may be able to help you. I discuss some potential advisors below.

Your Business Advisor

Friends, colleagues, mentors, college classmates, career counselors, former co-workers, current co-workers, old professors, gurus, wizened old geezers … all of these and more might serve as your business advisors. Informational interviews

– interviewing to see if you might like the job – can be valuable. But probably more valuable are friends, colleagues, and professionals on your side to give you human, business, pro-you, considered advice.

Hire a Lawyer if You Need One

One bad part of my job is sometimes having to deal with entrepreneurs and executives who hate lawyers. They hate lawyers because lawyers cost money. They hate lawyers because many lawyers slow down deals. They hate lawyers because countless lawyers argue too much. They hate lawyers for many reasons. Sometimes entrepreneurs and executives hate lawyers simply because they're cheap, parsimonious, miserly, or however you want to describe it. If the entrepreneur or executive is nasty about it, then I don't represent them, not ever.

However, there's a number of interesting, fun, "lawyer-hating entrepreneurs and executives" who are happy to tell you how they hate paying for lawyers. Indeed, they can be quite jovial about their distaste. These types try to avoid hiring lawyers whenever possible.

But the really shrewd ones know when they need a lawyer, and they pay good money for one. I've represented these kinds of lawyer-hating entrepreneurs and executives multiple times over the years.

Shrewd lawyer-hating entrepreneurs and executives hire lawyers when they recognize that they don't know the answers to all the questions, including questions like: Do you know everything about the laws that affect your employment? Do you know the ins and outs of an employment offer letter or employment contract? Do you know when, or even how, to protect yourself and your family via the contracting process? Do you know how badly the contract you are looking at can hurt you personally?

Rather, they know they require some good legal advice. That's why shrewd lawyer-hating entrepreneurs and executives hire a lawyer. You should probably too.

If you're lucky, your lawyer might even be able to give you good business advice. It has happened many times.

Hiring a lawyer may be expensive. The lawyer's fee comes out of your pocket (unless your prospective employer agrees to pay – more in later chapters about this). But hiring a lawyer may be the best investment you ever make. And it may not pay off until the ax falls years later and you're out on the street.

Your Lawyer Therapist

If you have a really good entrepreneur and executive employment lawyer, then he probably doubles as an amateur therapist. That's, in part, because, whatever your situation, he's probably seen your type of experience before.

And when you're under stress or being mistreated (hopefully it'll never happen!), you've got to tell your lawyer everything. If you're about to be fired or have just been fired, it may be the first time you've been professionally mistreated and faced "professional failure." When you're hurt (and hopefully you'll never be hurt!), especially if you've been blindsided or just don't understand why, you may need hand holding as much as you require excellent legal advice. Good employment attorneys salve many a wound.

Sometimes executives and entrepreneurs call asking how they can get themselves fired. They typically want to collect on pre-negotiated professional prenuptial agreements (accelerated vesting and cash!) and diversify (go to work for another company). Nevertheless, only a few executives and entrepreneurs enjoy being fired, even when they want to be fired. In other words, on firing day, no matter how great the golden handshake and no matter how rich, few executives and entrepreneurs enjoy the ax. They often like to talk to their understanding attorney.

So, consider retaining the amateur therapist masquerading as a lawyer. The conversation might help!

Make Sure You Hear What's Being Said

Researchers know that we only remember about 20% of what we hear. That means we only really hear 20% of what is said. Need I say more?

Genius, are You? All Powerful, are You? Did You Say You're a Professional Negotiator?

Are you a plenipotentiary of the United States of America with years of high stakes negotiations under your belt? Do you know everyone who is anybody? Are you a genius?

You are! You do! Fantastic!

But so what? Have you ever negotiated the definition of Cause? Do you know what single trigger refers to in an employment agreement? Ever read the 409A regs?

Consider consulting someone to assist you.

Hire Your Own Tax Advisor If You Need One

When you contemplate your comp, you're probably going to ask: "Will I be taxed?"

On the flip side, your employer wants to know: "Do I get a deduction for the comp package I'm paying?"

Your accountant or tax lawyer will tell you how and when you'll be taxed, or in grey areas, the risks of not paying various taxes. Similarly, your employer's tax advisors will advise your employer when and how it can take a deduction and when it'll be taxed.

In complex transactions – for example, when your employer is sold – tax experts sometimes drive decisions because changing the structure of a deal may fundamentally alter the amount of tax one party or the other will owe, and thus, ultimately what you'll receive in your pocket. In complex transactions, you the entrepreneur or executive may require a tax adviser.

Don't rely on your dependable long-time accountant if he doesn't know everything about the sophisticated transaction being contemplated. Lack of experience can equal millions of lost dollars.

Similarly, don't rely on your employer's tax specialist for tax advice. She advises your employer, not you. This means her job is to look out for your employer, not for you.

If you need a tax advisor, retain your own one. You should have a tax advisor who is loyal to you, and only you.

Things to Remember:

- Before founding a company, accepting funding, or beginning your job search, consider everything, including who you are and your personality and the personalities of everyone around you.
- If you need assistance in the entrepreneurial and executive world, then get help.
- Business advisors and lawyers may be able to assist you.
- Make sure you hear what's being said.
- Hire your own tax advisor if you need one.

5

Documents to Love & Hate

Rock Solid

"All I know is what my assistants told me and what's in your offer letter," I began. "You are negotiating a CEO contract for a shipping company of some sort and you're supposed to make $650,000 a year, with a 50% target bonus and get 10% ownership in the company over seven years. That's all I know."

Sinclair exclaimed, "Peterson and I have been discussing this deal for months, and..."

"Stop! You've been living this for months. But I'm new to this. I have no idea what's going on. Let's step back. Who is Peterson, what does he do, and what did he promise you?"

"Peterson is the majority partner and chairman of P-J-B Lines. He's had some health issues and is looking for someone to run the business."

"What kind of shipping does P-J-B Lines do?"

"It owns ships and ships cargo, principally between South and North America, but sometimes also to Europe. It owns the market in some places. Gross revenue is about $750 million plus or minus a year. It's a gargantuan cash cow."

"Why does Peterson want to hire you?"

"Because I've been in the shipping business for more than two decades and know what to do. Plus, he knows me and I'm honest."

"So why are you so pissed off? The offer letter says you'll make $650,000 a year in salary, $325,000 in bonus at target and will vest in more than 1% of P-J-B's equity each year for the next seven years. I assume the equity is the big upside."

"Yes, it could be worth $50 million or more. For months, Peterson has promised me an employment agreement when we are done negotiating the business terms. Yesterday, he sent me the two pager I sent you. Nothing like what I expected. I hope this hasn't all been a waste of time."

"So, what is it you want that's not in the offer letter?"

"I want a year's severance and bonus if they fire me."

"Do you want a year's paid COBRA medical insurance?

"Sure, why not?"

"What about a year's accelerated vesting on your equity?"

"Can I get that?"

"You can get whatever Petersen agrees to. If he approves, the agreement can go in an offer letter just the same as a full-blown employment agreement, and it's just as binding."

"Are you sure?"

"One sentence might do the trick. Something like, 'In the event the Company terminates Executive's employment for any reason, the Company shall pay Executive, in one lump sum, $975,000, less legally required withholding, pay Executive's COBRA premiums directly to the COBRA administrator for 12 months, and accelerate the vesting of Executive's option by one year so that on the employment termination date, Executive will be fully vested in that number of shares of the Company's common stock as Executive would have vested had Executive's last day of employment been the one year anniversary of Executive's actual last day of employment.'"

"That's what I want!"

"You also need protection if you have Good Reason to resign, sometimes called, a 'constructive quit.' If you're mistreated in any way, for example your salary is reduced or you're assigned to work on the docks, you should have the right to resign and receive your separation package. A Good Reason clause will take more than one sentence, but can still go in an offer letter. It doesn't matter how long your agreement is. It matters what's in the agreement,"

"What about all the other stuff that's in an employment contract?"

"There's lots of other stuff that you can ask for and lots of other clauses you can have in a full-blown employment agreement, but what really matters to you? Protecting your equity because yours is an equity play, and a year's pay and bonus, right?"

"Right."

"I don't know enough about what's going on yet, but if a two- or three-page offer letter makes Peterson happy, and you're happy with the equity protection and the severance in the offer letter, you don't need a 10-page agreement. If you want to spend negotiating capital on other things, the short offer letter should do the trick."

"One year's acceleration is north of $6 million so if you get me that and a year's severance and bonus, I don't care how long the contract is."

The Offer Letter v. The Employment Agreement

Offer letters and employment agreements describe your position and compensation. If you're smart, or shrewd, or lucky, or any of these in combination, *they are your professional prenuptial agreement*!

Most protective employment agreements and offer letters in at-will states are nothing more than severance agreements negotiated on day one.

How important is the professional prenuptial agreement? The answer depends on how important it is to you to protect yourself. Or to protect your equity. Or cashflow. Or other things that are important to you, for example, company-paid medical insurance.

Don't waste time worrying about whether your would-be employer gives you an offer letter or an employment agreement. What is *in* the offer letter or employment agreement matters, *not* how many pages the document is. A contract is a contract. A two-page offer letter can give you much more protection than the longest employment agreement.

Consider, for example, a two-page offer letter with one sentence you insert that says: "If your employment is terminated by our great Company for any reason, our great Company will accelerate the vesting of all unvested shares subject to all of your employee stock options."

Compare this to the twelve-page employment agreement that spends half-a-page defining "Cause," and then provides: "If our great Company terminates your employment without Cause, then our great Company will accelerate the vesting of 25% of the unvested shares subject to your employee stock option."

If you care mostly about protecting your equity, which document would you rather sign?

The two-page offer letter, of course. Why? Because:

- In the two-page letter, your employer's reason for firing you does not matter – you qualify for accelerated vesting whatever reason your employer gives for firing you. By contrast, under the twelve-page employment agreement, your employer can fire you for "Cause," however Cause is defined, and you get no accelerated vesting.
- The offer letter provides that you receive full accelerated vesting if your employer fires you. By contrast, the employment agreement provides only 25% accelerated vesting of your then unvested shares. So, if you are fired without Cause eight months into a 100,000-share

four-year option with a one-year cliff vesting clause, the offer letter ensures you receive an option to purchase 100,000 accelerated shares, the employment agreement only 25,000.

- Under the offer letter, the acceleration applies to *all* of your employee stock options, whether the Company granted the options at the start of your employment or sometime later. By contrast, under the employment agreement, only your initial option vests – that's the option granted in connection with the beginning of your employment.

The offer letters I really love are those that say they're not a contract even though they set out your comp, equity and benefits. If you and your employer execute the offer letter that says it's not a contract, then the offer letter is a contract for whatever you and the employer agreed to in writing.

Shortchanged

"What did U file a complaint for?" a lawyer I've known for years texted me.

"What case?" I texted back.

"Nibbles v. Clanbarker," came the reply.

"Come on Lloyd, Clanbarker wouldn't pay Nibbles the commissions he is owed," I texted.

"U could've called me. We just had lunch," Lloyd texted.

"No idea U represented them. They owe commissions. Commissions are wages, U know that," I replied.

"Message is loud and clear," Lloyd texted. "I told client if Nibbles wins a dollar, he gets attorneys' fees by statute, and U R expensive. I told client if it wins everything, it will never get fees."

"At least you give good advice," I texted back.

"What do you think about mediation?" Lloyd texted.

Living and Dying by Commission and Bonus Plans

What's the difference between a commission plan and a bonus plan? Sometimes not much.

Generally, commission plans involve payments based on sales, whereas, bonus plans pay based on many different types of metrics (or sometimes they are completely discretionary).

If you're in sales, you'll probably earn commissions on your sales, assuming you sell the amounts necessary to trigger the commissions.

The commission plan describes the commissions you may earn and the conditions under which you earn them. Commissions may be paid on any type of sale, from tires, to software, to services, to cars, to computer chips, to hot air balloons.

Make sure your employer gives you a commission plan *in writing*. Make sure you sign it (or accept it via email or another traceable medium if your state allows that type of acceptance – check with a lawyer to make sure).

Some sales superstars spend their careers searching for strong up and coming companies with *uncapped* commission plans, probably the holy grail of commission plans.

Uncapped plans mean the more you sell, the more you earn, with no limit. If the product is a good one, and you know what you're doing, you can earn more than the CEO with an uncapped plan. So, if you work under a plan that pays 5% of all sales, then you earn $50,000 on one million in sales, $500,000 on $10 million in sales and $5 million on $100,000,000 in sales. The sky is the limit.

But there is usually a cycle to companies and their uncapped plans. Often what happens is that when you earn "too much" for too many quarters, the manager running the business – sometimes an MBA who takes lesser risks – becomes jealous and puts in place a capped commission plan. And the most talented often move on.

It always amazes me how some companies don't like to pay the commissions they're bound to pay. It seems so short-sighted. Employees earning good commissions drive revenue and are likely to find jobs elsewhere if they're cheated out of pay. Nevertheless, commission disputes happen all the time.

Beware – some states allow your employer to change or cancel your commission plan mid-year, although generally benefits already accrued cannot be cancelled. Nefarious employers, however, will "interpret" their plans in ways that hurt you, which is how disputes often arise.

Other times, malcontents will fire you after the end of the commission period, but before the commission is paid, and then assert that you must be employed on the day you're paid to receive your commission.

Make sure your commission plan is clear as day to understand. Clear wording, clear commission triggers, lead to fewer disputes. Make sure too that your commission plan says that your commission is earned and payable as of the day you hit the triggering milestone or, at least, the last day of the commission period, even if the payment is made at a later time.

For their part, bonus plans often ground extra pay on objectives, metrics, or milestones. These milestones could be company sales or revenue. But they can also be so much more. Generally, the employer pays a certain sum when a metric is triggered.

Other bonus plans are completely discretionary. Still others have both a discretionary and objective component.

As with commission plans, make sure you thoroughly understand your bonus plan. Words matter. Also, make sure your employer gives you the bonus plan in writing. And that you accept it in writing.

And if your bonus plan is based on objectives, metrics or milestones, make sure whatever is triggering your bonus is clear and easily ascertained or measured. You ward off disputes with plainly written bonus plans plus bonus triggers that everyone can tell you either meet or don't meet.

The IPO

"Let's just bid one point nine million. The in-law unit is perfect for my parents," Polgar said to his wife Claire as they pushed their six-month old's stroller on a walk around the neighborhood. Polgar worked long hours at a start-up designing mobile internet games. Claire did the same at an internet security company. Polgar's parents had been taking care of their son, and the in-law unit would make child care easier.

"But that's four hundred thousand dollars over asking," Claire protested.

"Come on, Claire! How much did we net when we exercised your options and sold your stock two weeks ago after that odious six-month IPO lock-up expired?"

"Two point four million dollars. And we only sold fifty percent of your stock. What's an extra four hundred K?"

"This house is what we've been looking for and I'm worried one of the other, how many, count them, 58 new millionaires from your company, will bid on this house? Plus, besides being perfect for my parents, we work so hard that we don't have the time to keep looking."

"I know at least 40 of the 58 had less stock than I did, and I don't think any of them will be bidding on this house."

"Are you sure? Four hundred thousand dollars over asking is affordable for us. We can buy the whole house for cash if we want to and still have five hundred thousand in cash left over. And we still own fifty percent of your stock, which means we can exercise the stock option and sell tomorrow and net another two point four mil. Plus, hopefully, my stock will be worth more someday."

"Your parents are going to choke if they ever find out. Their store isn't worth four hundred thousand total and they've worked their entire lives at the store."

"When I was growing up, I never dreamed I would have this kind of money. It seems like four hundred K over asking is throwing away money."

"Not with all these people bidding over asking. And not if it gets us what we need. We got incredibly lucky with your company. Hopefully, we'll get lucky with mine. My parents are really going to love living so close to their grandson, you know that."

"Besides, we aren't my parents, are we? You're a vibrant twenty-eight-year-old risk taker with a college degree and two point four million dollars cash in the bank, another two point four million dollars after taxes in stock options."

"And I've got more stock options than you do, which could be worth a fortune if my company ever goes public."

Plus, we have a whole lifetime ahead of us to earn more.

"If you're really sure about this," Claire replied, "then we can tell the agent one point nine tonight."

The Path to Enrichment Through Equity

If you work for equity in the right company (stock price goes up and up and up), you could get rich, sometimes richer than you ever imagined, sometimes richer than all of your relatives that ever lived put together. When you hear on the news about an executive getting fired and leaving with millions, it's usually because the fired executive had equity grants.

Consider the following: If you work for 100,000 shares of common stock in your private employer, the company goes public, you bought those shares for $1 a share and then you sell the shares for $11/share, you just made a million dollars.

Here's the calculation: 100,000 shares x $11/share = $1,100,000 sales price, but then you subtract the cost of the shares, which is 100,000 shares x $1/share = $100,000, leaving you with $1,100,000 - $100,000 = $1,000,000 (all of this is before taxes, of course).

If you're able to sell the same shares for $21/share, you make $2 million. $31/share, 3 million.

On the other hand, if you work for a publicly traded multinational and you negotiate for an option to purchase 50,000 shares of your employer's common stock, and you joined the company when it's trading at $35 per share, work hard, vest, exercise the option for the shares, and then sell the shares when the stock is at $135 per share, you just made $5,000,000 (before taxes).

The calculation is: 50,000 shares multiplied by the difference between the per share sale price and your per share cost to buy those shares, which in this example is $135 - $35 = $100. 50,000 x $100 = $5,000,000.

Now let's say your public employer decides to grant you 50,000 shares of restricted stock over four years, deliverable in four tranches, at the first four anniversaries of your employment.

The restricted stock is like money. When it is delivered, it has a cash value, the amount the stock is trading for on the market. If the stock is trading at $50/share, on the first anniversary of your employment, you'll receive stock worth $625,000 (before taxes). You don't have to worry about paying for the stock – it just winds up in your account (less probably some or all of the taxes you owe on the income).

The calculation is: 12,500 shares (1/4 of the 50,000 share grant) x $50/share = $625,000 (before taxes).

This is the power of equity in public companies and private companies going public.

When private companies sell, whether privately or to public companies, the power of equity may also be evident.

For example, if you work for 100,000 shares of common stock in your private employer as in the example above, and your company sells to a private acquirer for $11/share in cash, you just made a million dollars (100,000 shares x $11/share less 100,000 x $1/share purchase price). If, instead, your private employer sells to a publicly traded acquirer for $11 of the public acquirer's stock for every share of your private employer's stock, and you sell your new shares, you just made a million dollars.

Stock options and restricted stock units (RSUs for short) are often the focus for those in the equity game in places like Silicon Valley, San Diego, Boston, Austin, and Raleigh Durham. But equity plays have made people like you rich in lots of places.

Even though many want equity, I can't tell you how many clients I've worked with who, when they first called, had no idea how stock options or RSUs work. And some of these clients are among the shrewdest executives and entrepreneurs around. Fluency in business does not necessarily make one facile with equity.

At least the equity neophytes can be educated.

Worse: Many I've met over the years have *never* read their equity agreements. And even among those who've read their equity agreements, a good percentage didn't understand them.

One big problem for those who read their agreements (and obviously for those who don't): The legalese can really hurt you, such as it did for all the poor employees losing their options in the "Both Ends of the Spectrum" Executive and Entrepreneur Story two chapters ago.

A second big problem: Lack of perspective, lack of experience. If you've always received kudos in life, you'll probably assume that will continue, and professional prenuptial protection is not that important.

Similarly, if you have not seen those entrepreneurs, executives, and everyday employees, *just like you*, who have been screwed, you probably don't have an appreciation for how bad it can be.

You really should read every boring word of every one of your equity agreements *before* you sign them. You also should get someone to help you understand *every word* you're not sure about.

Even with words and agreements you think you understand, if you're not seasoned in the risks you face (the ways you can be screwed), you should get someone with experience to educate you.

Stock options granted pursuant to a U.S. Internal Revenue Code qualified plan (that's most of them) usually contain three parts: notice of stock option grant; stock option agreement; and, equity plan.

Restricted stock granted pursuant to a qualified plan (often the same qualified plan under which stock options are granted) usually feature three components as well: notice of restricted stock [unit] grant; restricted stock [unit] agreement; and, equity plan.

I cover some of the ins and outs of these agreements in later chapters. The equity agreements I write about are the stock options and restricted stock agreements or restricted stock unit agreements (treated as one here) just described. I do so because they are probably the most well-known of employer, entrepreneur, and executive equity agreements.

However, there are definitely other employee equity agreements that can earn you a fortune. For example, profits interests in limited liability companies sometimes bring astronomical wealth to employees. Profits interests are percentage interests in the granting limited liability company's future profit stream. If those profits are strong, the profits interests may pay off.

Beware! Equity grants do not always have an upside. Many an employee can paper his walls with worthless stock certificates and stock options received from employers.

In the examples above of the 100,000 shares granted at $1/share, if you work for that employer for 10 years and your employer goes belly up, you have nothing but wallpaper. And in return for the failed "equity play," you probably accepted a lower-than-market base salary and bonus for the 10 years, meaning you earned substantially less over the decade than you could have elsewhere.

Similarly, if you vested in 50,000 shares at a purchase price of $35 per share as in the example above, and the shares spend the next nine years trading in the $10 - $20 per share range, your option is underwater for nine years, meaning you'll drown if you exercise it because you'll lose money.

How do you lose money? If you pay $35 per share for each of your vested shares, but you are only able to sell each share for $20 per share, for each share you exercise, you lose $15 per share.

And then there are the true disasters, where you might owe more than you earn in equity. For example, you borrow $100,000 from your employer in a full-recourse loan to purchase 100,000 shares of stock at $1.00 share (a full-recourse loan means the employer can collect on any of your assets if you don't repay the note). You do this because if you hold the stock for one year, you will owe only capital gains taxes on the stock gain, not ordinary income taxes. Depending on your tax bracket, the difference could save you 17% or more in federal taxes.

You expect your employer to do well, and plan to pay off the $100,000 note once you sell your stock. But, if your employer goes bankrupt, you won't have anything with which to pay off the note.

The bankruptcy trustee – whose job it is to collect as much as possible for the bankrupt and its creditors – will probably insist you repay the $100,000 note. Has this ever happened? Many times. Even more so, when the economy is weak. Hopefully you borrowed the money knowing the risks you faced, and understood, at the outset, that you were making a business bet that might turn out to be a loser.

What Did You Say?

"Do I really have to negotiate the confidentiality agreement?" Amanda Escobar asked plaintively.

Amanda was negotiating for a high-profile CFO position at a Fortune 100 company, a position that pays millions.

"You're going in as CFO. It's your job to criticize whatever you see financially that needs to be criticized," I responded.

"You may have to fire people or give them bad reviews. You may even need to go directly to the audit committee to report the CEO, EVP of World Wide Sales or others for wrongdoing. You know that."

"They can't stop me from doing any of those things," Amanda said. This wasn't her first public company.

"But the non-disparagement clause in the confidentiality agreement says you can't disparage the company or any of its employees while you're employed. Non-disparagement means anything that puts another in a bad light, even if the statements are one hundred percent true. A non-disparagement obligation after your employment terminates is one thing. But not while you are employed. And I have to tell you, companies hate changing their confidentiality agreements, because they are like vetted forms to them."

"What if I sign as is, and just ignore it?" Amanda asked.

"If you do that, I'll write you an email that says I'm 'CYAing' myself, and that I advise you to write an email to the CEO or Board to ask permission every time you want to disparage the Company or any employee or any product or anything associated with the Company. That's the best way to protect yourself if you agree to the non-disparagement clause, as is."

Gotcha – The Confidentiality Agreement

You, like so many employees, have probably never read your employer's confidential information and invention assignment agreement, CIIAA for short. CIIAAs are usually dense legalese. Sometimes, you must read them multiple times to understand them. I hate reading them and I practice in the field.

Your CIIAA might be called something else (it might have a different title). One employer might call your CIIAA a "confidentiality agreement." Another might label it a "proprietary information agreement." Some even call their CIIAAs "employment agreements." All are referred to here as CIIAAs.

The primary intent of a CIIAA is to protect your employer's intellectual property (IP) by contract and to make sure whatever you invent or create while working for your employer belongs to your employer. Your CIIAA undoubtedly provides that you can't disclose your employer's IP and you assign all the IP you created to your employer.

Various state and federal laws, including states' trade secrets acts, make it illegal for you to use a former employer's proprietary information and trade secrets for any purpose other than for the former employer. The CIIAA is an attempt to broaden these statutory IP protections by contract – you sign, the employer signs, and there's a contract.

Unfortunately, your CIIAA is a "must read." CIAAs often contain "gotchas," clauses you would never suspect would be included in an agreement intended to protect IP. For example, many CIIAAs contain a clause requiring you not to solicit your employer's employees or consultants to another business once your employment ends. What part of the title of Confidential Information and Invention Assignment Agreement says anything about non-solicitation obligations?

Your CIIAA may also contain a non-disparagement clause. Or an arbitration clause. Sometimes it contains a non-competition clause. Sometimes an at-will employment clause. Sometimes a clawback clause. And much more. Ignore reading them at your peril.

Generally, employers abhor negotiating changes to any part of their CIIAAs and often resist every attempt to do so. If you're joining a new employer as anything other than a C-Suite officer, there's little chance your would-be employer will make any modifications to its CIIAA for you, no matter how hard you try.

However, if you're joining a new employer as a C-Suite officer, the CIIAA may contain terms that, literally read, will make it impossible for you to do your job. One example is a CIIAA non-disparagement clause that prohibits you from saying anything negative, no matter how truthful, about your employer or its employees while you are employed. There is no way you can do a C-Suite officer's job with a restriction like that.

Another example is a CIIAA clause that prohibits you from disclosing any of your employer's IP without the express written consent of the company. If you're joining as CEO, your job will be to decide when to disclose, and when not to disclose, your employer's IP. You shouldn't have to get the Board's permission every time you want to do so. If you disclose the company's IP, and the Board doesn't like what you've done, the Board can fire you. But it's your job to run your company until that happens and your CIIAA shouldn't hinder you from doing so (nor should it provide the Board with an easy excuse to fire you for breach of the CIIAA).

If the CIIAA contains terms that will make it impossible for you to do your job, then you should discuss revising those terms (for you specifically) before you join your would-be employer, even if it is unhappy with the conversation. If your would-be employer makes the necessary changes, great. If not and you take the position, you may be left with the choice of either breaching the CIIAA as you do your job, or taking laborious self-protective measures, such as obtaining Board permission every time you decide to do something that might breach the CIIAA.

Things to Remember:

- It doesn't matter whether it's called an "offer letter" or an "employment agreement." What matters are the protections written in the document.
- Make sure your commission or bonus plan is as clear as day, and in writing.
- If you have a commission or bonus plan with metrics, milestones or objectives, make sure whatever is triggering payment is easily ascertained or measured.
- Receiving equity in a company can sometimes enrich you.
- Make sure you know the risks in your equity agreements before you agree to them.
- Read your confidentiality agreement before you sign it. Beware of any "gotchas" it may contain.

6

More Documents to Love & Hate

Summit Lee!

"Don't get ripped off like I did in my first turnaround," Summit Lee said to her mentee Greg Barnberger over lunch at her favorite Italian restaurant.

"If you're going to be a turnaround artist, you need to negotiate a guaranteed payday at the beginning. Once the change in control happens, all those investors you made rich won't be around anymore, and you don't want to get left holding the bag."

Summit is a preeminent turnaround specialist, and always incisively to the point. Greg felt lucky, and privileged, to call her his mentor. He had sought Summit's advice because he recently received a job offer to be CEO of a struggling private-equity-backed company.

"What does your offer letter say happens if the company is sold? You just told me your equity vests over four years and you're going in to package up the place for a sale." Summit stopped to take a bite of her eggplant parmigiana. Summit judged Italian restaurants by their eggplant parmigiana.

"They gave me a year severance if they terminate me without cause."

Summit took a sip of her chianti. "What about accelerated vesting of your unvested equity?" she asked.

"There's nothing in the offer letter about that."

"Greg, the first thing you should negotiate for is accelerated vesting of some or all of your unvested equity if your employment is terminated by your employer without cause or by you for good reason, whether or not there is a change in control. Believe you me, that will protect you whenever someone thinks you're not doing a good job."

"Speaking of change in control, how long do you think it will take for you to sell the company?"

"A year and a half to three years, depending on how things play out," Greg replied.

"This is an equity play for you isn't it?" Summit asked.

"It's all about equity," Greg agreed.

"Then don't get ripped off like I did the first time. I turned my first company around and sold it after only two years, but my equity vested pro-rata over four years. Stupidly, I didn't protect my equity. The acquirer fired me within weeks after the closing of the sale and I lost millions."

"What do you think I should do?"

"Unless you negotiate for full accelerated vesting whether or not there is a change in control, what you need is a change in control clause in your offer letter that says if the company terminates your employment in anticipation of, on or at any point after a corporate change in control, or you have good reason to quit, or if the company or a purchaser ever attempt to terminate your option while you're employed, one hundred percent of all unvested shares subject to your stock option will immediately vest."

"Is that market?" Greg asked.

"It's definitely market, but even if it weren't, it's certainly a commercially reasonable ask. And the private equity guys who made you the offer are going to know that. Plus, if you turn around the company within three years, whatever the investors pay you will be a pittance of what they walk away with."

"You should also ask for partial or full acceleration of your equity at the closing of a change in control, whether or not your employment is terminated. That way you receive an immediate upside if you do what you're being hired to do."

"One thing to look out for is a change in control clause that expires one year after the closing. After I got ripped off the first time, my lawyer turned me on to this hidden way to hurt you."

"What's this about?" Greg asked.

"Let's say you're really good and sell the company after eighteen months. And let's say you negotiate one year of accelerated vesting if the company terminates your employment without cause at any time, and full accelerated vesting if the company terminates your employment without cause during the first year after a change in control. If this happens and if the company terminates your employment one year and one day after the closing, at 30 months, and you get one year of accelerated vesting, then you'll have a total of 42 months of vesting. You'd lose six months' worth of vesting. If you don't negotiate for accelerated vesting, you would lose eighteen months of equity."

"Do you think they'll give me protection on all of this?"

"If they don't, turn around another company!"

Potential Gold – The Change in Control Agreement

Your change in control agreement describes what you'll receive, if anything, if your employer undergoes a corporate change in control.

A corporate change in control generally occurs when whoever or whatever ultimately controls your employer or its assets changes. Selling one company to another company is a classic way the sold company undergoes a change in control. Other ways may include a change in the majority of the Board, an initial public offering, or an exclusive licensing of most or all of your employer's assets to a third party.

Change in control agreements define what constitutes a change in control, and once triggered, the benefits you will receive.

Change in control agreements can be very lucrative, particularly when they involve the accelerated vesting of equity or when they call for significant cash payments.

The Triggers!

If you know something about professional prenuptial protection, then you probably know about "single trigger" and "double trigger" agreements.

However, "single trigger" and "double trigger" mean different things, depending on what you're talking about.

When you're talking about an employment agreement or offer letter, and you're talking about "double trigger" protection, the first trigger is usually a change in control, and the second trigger, termination of your employment. If your offer letter provides double trigger protection, then you'll receive whatever the benefits are only if your employer has undergone a change in control (first trigger is the change in control), *and* thereafter, your employer terminates your employment (second trigger is termination of employment), often within a specified time period. If your employer terminates your employment before undergoing a change in control, you receive no separation benefits.

But, if you have "single trigger" protection in your offer letter, that usually means you'll receive separation benefits if your employment is terminated (first trigger is termination of employment), without regard to whether your employer undergoes a change in control.

When you're talking about a change in control agreement (or a change in control clause in an employment agreement/offer letter), however, the first trigger is usually the change in control itself. Thus, if you are protected by a "single trigger" change in control agreement, then you receive whatever benefits are spelled out in the contract *as soon as* your employer undergoes a change in control.

"Double trigger" change in control protection in your change in control agreement usually means the same thing as double trigger protection in your offer letter: your employer must undergo a change in control (first trigger), and thereafter, must terminate your employment (second trigger). Only then will you receive benefits.

The most pro-you combination is single trigger protection on termination of employment and single trigger protection in the event of a change in control. With this combo, you receive benefits if your employment is terminated *or* if your employer undergoes a change in control while you're employed.

What are the Liquidation Preferences?

"Do you know what the company's liquidation preferences are, if they have any?" Summit asked just after she and Greg ordered the world's best cannolis for dessert.

"No," Greg admitted.

"You need to find out. You'd be a total fool not to. I know a few who've really been wrecked by preferences."

"Look, you're planning on selling the company in one-and-a-half to three years. If you sell below liquidation preferences, sometimes called the overhang, all the purchase price will go to the preferred stockholders, and nothing to the common stockholders. Since your stock option will be for common stock, you'll get nothing if the sale is below liquidation preferences."

"I definitely don't want that to happen," Greg said.

"What you need is a management carve out agreement that guarantees you, and maybe others on your management team, a certain percentage of the sales price if the company sells below preferences," Summit explained.

"How does that work?" Greg asked.

"I'm making up these numbers because you don't know what the preferences are and you haven't told me what you think you can sell the company for, but let's say you sell the company for $100,000,000, but the preferences are $150,000,000, then you'll get nothing."

"But if you have a management carve out agreement, that guarantees you 5% of the sales price if the company sells for between $50 million and $100,000,000 and 8% of the sales price if the company sells for more than $100,000,000, you'll do alright."

"If you sell the company above preferences, the management carve out will be reduced by any amount you receive for your equity, but you'll have protected your downside unless you have to offload the company in a fire sale," Summit explained as the cannolis arrived.

Backstop to Gold – The Management Carve Out Agreement

If you're an executive at a poorly performing company that should be sold, you might consider working elsewhere. No reason to stick around a sinking ship, especially if you have a significant amount of underwater equity (the value of your equity is lower than the price you must pay to buy the equity) that will never be worth anything. Similarly, you might be working at a publicly traded company on the downward slide to oblivion.

If you're a C-Suite executive or entrepreneur-in-demand, one way to protect yourself against an equity zero is to negotiate for a "management carve out agreement." Although there are many types of management carve out agreements, generally, they reserve some portion of the sales price for you the CEO, or you the management team, or you some other important corporate player. Often, they only reserve an amount if your employer's sale is above a minimum price.

It's like a commission on the sale of your company or a bonus with triggers based on your employer's sales price. Your management carve-out agreement, for example, might guarantee you and the other key corporate players 5% of the sales price of your employer if your employer sells for over $25 million, 8% if the sales price exceeds $50 million, and 10% if the sales price is north of $100 million.

Working at a private start-up that has high liquidation preferences (a big overhang) is another reason why you might want a management carve-out agreement. As discussed in the Executive and Entrepreneur Story above and as explained in greater detail two chapters hence, without a management carve out agreement or other protective measures, liquidation preferences may cause every dollar of the sales price to be paid to the investors, with nothing going to you.

Why would your board of directors agree to a management carve-out agreement? Because the Board wants to sell your employer for top dollar, and it wants to incentivize you to do so!

It Hurts

"I got a great job offer from TileOne. It's one of the biggest tile distributors in the business. They want me to oversee sales to their national accounts," John Barnes said.

"They offered me twice what I'm making now," he explained. "I really want to take the job. It would be a big step up for me and my family. But I'm worried my former employer might come after me."

"Why are you worried?" I asked.

"I've been in sales with Wood Across America for the past eight years. When I started out at WAA, I signed a non-compete agreement that says I can't work for a competitor for a year."

"Do TileOne and WAA compete?

"In some areas. TileOne's and WAA's products can both be used in flooring, bathrooms, or kitchens."

"Did you sell in those areas at WAA?"

"Yes."

"Will you be selling in those areas at TileOne?"

"Somewhat. The thing is I'll be overseeing national accounts at TileOne. At WAA, I called directly on accounts."

"I'm not going to be able to get to the bottom of your situation until I read your non-compete agreement, so send it over to me. Without reading the words in your contract, and learning the details of what you do and did, I won't be able to give you any advice."

"It just doesn't seem fair that WAA can keep me from earning double what they pay me. WAA is a wood company. TileOne is all about tile. Why shouldn't I be able to provide more for my family?"

The Restrictive Non-Compete Agreement

A non-compete agreement is just that, an agreement that prohibits you from competing against your former employer, often for one or two years (and sometimes longer). They are legal in most states.

The non-compete agreements I discuss in this book are *employment-based* non-compete agreements. These are agreements that restrict you from competing with your employer after your employment terminates *simply because* you were an employee. These types of agreements differ from *transaction-based* non-compete agreements which prohibit you from competing as part of a transaction, often your sale of stock to an acquirer when your employer is sold.

States differ on how restrictive employment-based non-compete obligations may be. Some states will pretty much enforce a non-compete agreement against you even if you can't feed your family. Other states will modify or set aside the agreement if it is too onerous.

On the other hand, employment-based non-compete clauses and agreements are unenforceable, to one degree or another, in some states, and the list of states where they are unenforceable has recently been growing.

For example, employment-based non-compete agreements are unenforceable in California, Oklahoma, and North Dakota, although the states differ a bit on what they refuse to enforce. North Dakota and California will refuse to enforce a non-solicitation-of-customer clause. This clause attempts to prohibit you from soliciting the customers of your former employer. Oklahoma, however, enforces the clause.

In North Dakota and California, the CEO of a major chip manufacturer is free to quit her employer, and immediately walk across the street to begin running her former employer's major competitor. (Although, of course, restrictions abound preventing that CEO from using her former employer's confidential information in the process.)

On the other side of those states' borders, however, that same CEO could potentially be locked into a non-compete agreement prohibiting her from working for the competitor for a number of years.

It's Crooked

"What do you think about the arbitration clause?" Anderson Wang asked. He'd called to talk about the draft employment agreement he'd received.

"Arbitration is basically crooked," I responded.

"There are some good arbitrators out there," I continued, "but in my opinion too many are biased in favor of the big law firms and big companies because they are the repeat players and the arbitrators know where their bread is buttered. There's basically no appeal from an arbitration so you're one and done."

"Arbitration does have some upsides that might benefit you because you're an executive. Arbitration is confidential so nothing will get out in the public as with a lawsuit. It's usually faster to a resolution than a lawsuit. And with a straightforward contract claim, you might choose arbitration, especially if it's a binary contract, where either the contract is breached or it isn't breached."

"However, even with contracts, arbitrators are basically free to do what they want to do because there's no appeal. They can read a contract any way they want to read it. I've seen arbitrators decide that the words of a contract don't really mean what they say."

"Another question you should consider is how much negotiating capital you want to spend on the arbitration clause, especially when you have many other terms to negotiate."

"I'm going to let it go," Anderson replied. "I don't plan on having a dispute with them, and if I do, I'd rather it all be confidential."

"OK, what other questions do you have?"

Taking Away Your Right to a Jury Trial – The Arbitration Agreement

The arbitration agreement takes away your right to a jury trial. Plain and simple.

The arbitration agreement requires you to tell your tale of wrongdoing to a private person called an arbitrator (sometimes more than one arbitrator). Successfully appealing the arbitrator's decision is nearly impossible.

Your employer wants to take away your right to a jury trial because, generally speaking, arbitrations are more employer friendly, and arbitrators rarely award punitive damages, as juries sometimes do. In other words, your chance of winning, and your chances of winning more, are significantly reduced in arbitration as compared to most judicial systems.

Arbitrators tend to be pro-company for a number of reasons. Some are former judges. Former judges simply are not the common people and frequently impose their own limited view of what damages should be and who is and who is not credible. Judges come from a system where their job is to control juries (regular people) so their mindset is often to control the plaintiff (claimant in an arbitration) and control the award. Judges are also frequently well-off and pro-business.

As a whole, arbitrators are not in any sense a cross-section of the population you are entitled to when you bring your case to a jury. Arbitrators who are not former judges are usually highly educated lawyers.

Unfortunately, there is also the unseemly underbelly of arbitration. Many arbitrators tend to be pro-company, or pro-big-law firm because those are the repeat players in their arbitration world. Some of the big law firms, perhaps your employer's law firm, and some employers, bring many cases before the same arbitrator or arbitral authority. If the arbitrator does not rule in the repeat players' favor, that arbitrator probably won't be chosen to arbitrate for your employer or your employer's big law firm again; thus, that arbitrator will not make as much money as he or she would have had he or she ruled for the big company.

A retired judge once told me that he wished he could get more of some large company's arbitration business. Why? Because he could charge that company $600, $700, $800 or more per hour for the work. It's very difficult to be objective when your income depends on that kind of dough.

If you work for a significant size financial services firm, then you'll probably face a suspect FINRA (Financial Industry Regulatory Authority) arbitration panel. That's because your employment agreement probably requires you to arbitrate all disputes with your employer before FINRA.

Just as ordinary customers of broker-dealers are regularly victimized by the FINRA arbitration system that the financial institutions of the world (like you may be going up against) convinced Congress to establish, so too will you be facing an uphill battle. The number of repeat arbitrators in the FINRA system is extraordinary – these repeat arbitrators depend on broker-dealers to appoint them to arbitration panels. And they arbitrate over and over again.

All of this is not to say that you never want arbitration. If you have a straightforward contract dispute about commissions or stock ownership, for example, you might opt for arbitration. You hope that the arbitrator will make a straightforward decision regarding whether you earned your commissions or you didn't or whether you own the stock or you don't.

You might also opt for arbitration because you'll probably receive a faster result, because in a breach of contract dispute you aren't going to be awarded punitive damages, and because, in court, you may be required to try the case before a judge anyway. But still, you might need to contend with (lose at the hands of) an arbitrator who decides that the contract language does not mean what it says, and justifies whatever ruling he makes on the grounds that the contract must be read as a whole. It has happened many times.

Arbitration may also appeal to you because it is a private, confidential resolution of your dispute, whereas the court system is a public process.

Arbitration, however, can be expensive and you might not want to arbitrate because of the cost. Arbitrators are paid for their time by the parties. Judges are not. (Taxpayers pay their salaries.) And arbitral authorities frequently charge more than the judicial system in filing and administrative fees.

Some arbitrations strike me as full-service employment projects. Arbitrators have every financial incentive to request more and more briefing.

Fortunately, in some states, an employer cannot force an employee to arbitrate a case unless the employer pays for the arbitrator and the arbitral authority (but not attorneys' fees). This limits the cost of arbitration, and at least may make the process more affordable for you.

The Protective Indemnification Agreement

What happens if little ol' you are sued for something you did in the course and scope of your employment? Wouldn't you want your employer to defend you, pay your legal fees, and take a lot of the tension and worry out of the lawsuit? Most people would.

When your employer indemnifies you, your employer is obligated to do these things (depending on what the indemnification agreement says). Some states require indemnification for all employees by law. Others do not.

If you're a C-Suite executive or entrepreneur, you should demand a sweetheart indemnification agreement from your employer. The sweetheart indemnification agreement will require your employer to pay your attorneys' fees *in advance*, and only require you to pay anything if a third party finds that you are liable and acted in bad faith.

Note that some employers include indemnification rights for directors and certain officers or employees in their corporate governance documents (e.g. bylaws). Even if you're protected by these documents, you should confirm coverage in your offer letter or employment agreement to make your right to indemnification a right that flows directly to you by contract.

Employee Handbook & Company Policies

The employee handbook and company policies describe all your employer's rules and policies. Read them before you join your employer.

If there is anything in the employee handbook or company policies that you don't like or that conflicts with the terms of your offer letter or employment agreement (this is not uncommon), make sure your offer letter or employment agreement negates the terms at issue.

Back-End Separation (Severance) Agreement

If you didn't negotiate a professional prenuptial employment agreement on the front-end of your employment, there may still be hope.

You may be able to negotiate a separation (severance) agreement with your former employer, or soon-to-be former employer, at the back end of your employment relationship.

Separation agreements negotiated at the conclusion of employment may pay the departing employee money, provide COBRA/health coverage, accelerate the vesting of equity, deliver benefits, and much more. The separation package depends on the circumstances of each case. There are many reasons why employers give departing employees separation agreements when they are not required to do so.

One clause featured in almost every separation agreement is the release of the employer. Your employer or ex-employer wants you to release every possible claim under the sun you may have against your employer and all of its affiliates, other than those that the law prohibits you from releasing. In return for your release, your employer agrees to deliver whatever benefits you negotiate for and are described in the separation agreement. There's lots more about separation agreements later on in this book.

It's a Voting Agreement

"Can I really do that? Are you sure?" Ailatva Mas, Ph.D. asked. This was Ailatva's first start-up. She had created a predictive algorithm-driven software, and already had investors banging on her door.

"Yes, Ailatva, I'm sure. A voting rights agreement is just like any other contract. You can agree with Nibor Capital and Ile Funds that they'll vote all their Series A preferred stock for three Board members chosen by you."

"Nibor and Ile each want seats on your company's Board as part of their Series A investments, and given the dollars they're investing, you probably have to give them the seats."

"But you've got leverage! Ailatva Software Inc. is your company! You definitely want to keep control of your Board. And the way to do that is to enter into a voting rights agreement with Nibor and Ile whereby everyone agrees that your company will have a five-person Board, and all of your, Nibor's and Ile's shares will be voted for three Board members chosen by you, one Board member chosen by Nibor and one chosen by Ile."

"Wow. I didn't know anything about voting rights agreements. If I can get them to agree to vote their shares in other ways, can that go into a voting rights agreement too?"

"Yes, pretty much anything that's legal that you all agree to that has to do with voting stock can be put into a voting rights agreement."

Your Company's Stock and Funding Agreements

If you work for a corporation, it issues stock. If you work for a limited liability company, it issues units or interests or profits interests. An LLC can be organized so that it pretty much mimics a corporation's equity.

In this section, I discuss the funding and related agreements for corporations, the Inc.'s of the world.

Common stock is the basic, first level, of equity in a corporation. It may be the only type of stock in a corporation. In England, common stock is known as "ordinary shares."

Some companies have different classes of common stock. More than one class of common stock generally means that all common stock carries the same *equity* rights (all shares receive the same dividend if one is granted, the same payout if the company is sold, etc.), but the various classes of common stock carry different voting rights. For example, one class of common stock may vote ten votes per share of stock, whereas, another class of common stock might vote one vote per share of common stock.

Corporate employers such as yours typically issue common stock to their employees, officers, and directors. Sometimes, they grant employees stock options, restricted stock or RSUs for the delivery of common stock.

Some corporate employers feature different classes of stock, each of which probably carries different equity and voting rights. A public company thus may have B shares which carry with them whatever special equity and voting rights are described in the documents that created those shares.

Start-ups and private corporations often issue their investors, particularly sophisticated angel investors, venture capital investors, or private equity investors, preferred stock in return for the money they invest in the company. Preferred stock provides benefits and rights to these investors that are typically senior to the rights and benefits of common stock.

Start-ups and other private companies sometimes have more than one type of preferred stock. These "series" of preferred stock are often labeled with a name or letter to signify which series was issued first.

For example, your employer may have common stock for you and the company's other founders and employees, Series Seed preferred stock, Series A preferred stock, Series B preferred stock and Series C preferred stock. Very early investors, probably friends and family of the founders, and early angel investors purchased the Series Seed preferred stock.

After that, and over time, investors purchased more and more of the company. The next round of investors purchased Series A preferred stock. After that, your company sold and purchasers invested in Series B preferred stock, and thereafter, Series C preferred stock.

Hopefully your company's valuation increased with each financing round. If your company is not doing well, however, it may have had a flat financing round (e.g., the company's valuation did not change between the Series B and Series C financing rounds), or even a down round (e.g., your company's valuation decreased between the B and C round).

Even though Seed comes before A, A before B, and B before C, the *seniority* of the rights and preferences of your employer's preferred stock are usually in reverse order, meaning the later investors usually have rights and preferences either equal to or greater than the rights and preferences of the earlier investors.

So, in this example, if your employer is ever sold, the Series C preferred stock may have the right to receive their initial investment back from the sales price of your company before any other series of stock receives a penny of the sale proceeds.

Note that it is possible to put numbers after any series of preferred stock. So, for example, your employer may have Series D-1, Series D-2, and Series D-3 of preferred stock.

If you care about what your stock may be worth or about who controls your corporation, then you *must* learn all about the rights and preferences of all of the kinds of stock in your corporation. In other words, the rights and preferences in your employer's preferred stock purchase agreements (and other funding documents), may be absolutely critical for your financial happiness and wellbeing. You *must* read and understand them or ask your attorney (or other trusted advisor) to explain their terms to you.

The rights and preferences of all stock in your employer should be public information. They should be described in the corporation's certificate or articles of incorporation on file with the appropriate government authority for the company's state of incorporation. Public companies will disclose these rights in other places as well, for example, in their proxy statements.

The stock purchase agreements of your employer's funding rounds describe a lot of important information. This includes the price of the corporations' stock that is being sold, the total amount of money (called, "capital") investors will pay for the stock, the class of stock being sold, how much stock investors will receive in return for their payments, and the rights and preferences each share of stock carries.

Many financings in private companies are accompanied by an investor rights agreement. An investor rights agreement typically gives investors, your employer, and possibly you and your company's founders certain rights and commits you and them to various obligations and restrictions. For example, the investor rights agreement might say that if certain investors sell their stock in your employer those investors may require you and the other signatories to sell your shares (this is called a "drag-along" right).

Your employer's stockholders may also have voting rights agreements that requires whoever signed them to vote their shares in some pre-determined way. This might hamstring you as the entrepreneur or executive, especially if you've signed the voting agreements. On the positive side, a voting rights agreement may require all signatories to vote their shares to elect you (or someone else) to your employer's Board.

Some or all of the investors in your employer may have registration agreements, which obligate your employer to register the investors' shares for sale on a public stock exchange in certain situations. There are multiple flavors of registration rights. Some might require your employer to register the shares no matter what. Others would only do so in specific circumstances.

If your start-up ever runs out of money and, for one reason or another, cannot immediately raise the money it requires, your employer may negotiate a "bridge loan." Investors agree to "bridge" your employer from one funding round to another by loaning your employer money. Related is the convertible bridge loan, which allows the investor to convert the loan into stock at a value or event that the parties agree on before signing the convertible bridge loan.

A warrant is very similar to an employee stock option, but whoever or whatever owns the right in your company to exercise the contract (called a warrant in this case) at a specific price and receive delivery of stock is usually not required to be an employee or consultant of your employer. The warrant holder might be anyone, from investors, to landlords, to vendors, to you (possibly if you're also an investor, landlord or vendor).

In very early stage startups, investors may invest in a convertible loan or a SAFE, which is short for, "simple agreement for future equity."

Convertible loans are similar to bridge loans. They generally contain terms allowing the investor-promisor to convert loan principal and interest to equity at the closing of the startup's initial priced financing round (e.g., at the Series A financing). If a financing does not occur in whatever time period is set out in the convertible loan, the startup is obligated to repay the note.

The SAFE is a contract by which the investor "invests" money in a start-up, and in return, the start-up agrees to deliver stock to the SAFE holder when it receives the first funding that values the company.

If you're a founder with leverage, you probably want your investors investing in a SAFE, rather than a convertible note. SAFEs can be a very good deal for you the entrepreneur because your company does not have debt on its books and you're able to delay the valuation of your startup until a later time, hopefully after the enterprise has become more valuable. In this way, you the entrepreneur hopefully give up less stock in your company (less dilution) than if your investors had first invested in a low-priced initial seed financing.

To attract investors to invest in a SAFE, a SAFE usually contains a cap or a discount or both. The cap is the maximum amount of company value at which the SAFE investments convert into company equity. The discount is the amount of extra stock the investor receives in the initial financing round if the company's valuation falls at or below the cap (convertible loans may also contain caps and discounts).

Thus, a SAFE with a $20 million cap and 20% discount means if the first priced round of the company's equity is $40 million, the investor will receive that number of shares that the investor would have received if the valuation in the financing were $20 million (essentially, twice as many shares as the new investors). But, if the first round of financing values the corporation at $10 million (under the cap), then the SAFE investor receives 20% more in shares per dollar invested than do the others newly investing in the financing round.

Things to Remember:

- Change in control agreements can protect you if your employer is sold or otherwise undergoes a corporate change in control.
- Single trigger protection on termination of employment and single trigger protection on a change in control is the best combination of triggers for you the entrepreneur or executive.
- A management carve out agreement might protect you if your company is doing poorly or has high liquidation preferences.
- Watch out for non-compete and arbitration agreements.

- Enter into an indemnification agreement if you're able to do so (and know what protections your state or corporate governance documents provide, even if you're not able to negotiate for one).
- Know what's in your employee handbook & company policies.
- If you haven't negotiated a professional prenuptial employment agreement, there's always hope you can negotiate a back-end separation agreement.
- Your employer's funding agreements are critical – make sure you understand them all (get an advisor to help, if needed).

7

Big Picture Strategies

I Just Got Fired

"Tell me 'I told you so!' Go ahead. I'm never not listening to you again." Derfy shouted over the phone.

Not too many CFO's would go by "Derfy," but a beloved sister gave him the name when they were little. At 58, Derfy is a repeat CFO. He's raised hundreds of millions from venture capitalists and private equity funds over the years, sold two companies and brought one public. Until earlier in the day, Derfy had been Conti Design's CFO. Conti makes financial software.

"Three big exits with only half a screw-up before this one," I offered. "You've done pretty well without protection so far."

"I hate you." Derfy bellowed.

It's fair to say that Derfy hates lawyers. Judging by the number of times in the past twenty years he's called me, he likes me though. I think.

"Never again," Derfy continued.

"You know what they say?" I asked.

"No, what do they say, oh wise one?"

"Welcome to the NFL!" I answered.

"The NFL?" Derfy was momentarily confused. "What do you mean the NFL? The National Football League?"

"The big leagues," I responded. "People get fired in the big leagues!"

"That unethical, amoral, up-the-ass, piece of you know what. I just can't stand Dungman." Derfy was referring to Conti Design's CEO John Dungman. "I never want to see slurry-face ever again."

"What happened?"

"Dungman fired me by text. Can you believe it? I've never been fired before...and by text! A week before I get a big equity vest in my option. Slimy like a stepped-on slug, Dungman is."

"Did they give you a separation agreement?"

"Yeah. Two month's salary and COBRA. That's it."

"No accelerated vesting?"

"None. I'm going to tell you where all the bodies are buried so you can negotiate a good severance package for me, oh wise one."

"I know you hate Dungman, but you should negotiate your exit package yourself. Face-to-face."

"No way." Derfy was emphatic.

"Dungman is a turd, but you should negotiate face-to-face, coldly and calculatingly," I said assertively. "Not now though. Call me in a few days after you've had time to calm down. There's no rush."

"I want this done as soon as possible. I want to move on with my life."

"Not today. Calm down today. Celebrate your freedom. Call me Friday. You have to be cold and calculating, all the way to the bank."

"I hate Dungman. What an a-hole." Derfy exclaimed.

"Did you hear what I said?"

"Easier said than done. You didn't just get fired, and by text! Cold and calculating, it's not so easy."

"All the way to the bank! We'll talk turkey on Friday."

"You're getting me off the phone?

"Yes."

"I just got fired."

"Do you want me to tell you all this positive stuff, like how you'll probably be calling me in six months and telling me your firing is the best thing that ever happened to you? Call me on Friday."

"I hate you, oh wise one."

Negotiate Directly

You just got fired for incompetence. Your boss has been a passive-aggressive tyrant for months. Or maybe the guillotine wielder has been threatening to fire you for years.

You want a severance agreement. But damned if you'll negotiate with that dictator. You don't ever want to speak to him again, that's for sure. You think to yourself, "I'll hire Jotham to negotiate. He knows what he's doing."

I certainly know what I'm doing. But the great majority of the time, I'm going to tell you to go see the ex-boss who just fired you, grit your teeth, and make your ask. Do so assertively, but respectfully, coldly and calculatingly, and laugh all the way to the bank with your spoils.

Or maybe, the lead Board member just called you with the offer of a lifetime. You don't want to negotiate because you fear you might piss off the Board member, and you worry he might pull your offer. This, after all, is the job you've always wanted. CEO, the crème de la crème! You think, "I'll get Jotham to negotiate for me. He knows what he's doing."

I've got news for you. Most of the time, I'm going to tell you to negotiate the key terms of your CEO employment agreement directly with the Board member. If you negotiate assertively, but respectfully, you're more likely to expeditiously and smoothly achieve your goals. The Board member might also appreciate you all the more for it. At the end of the day, she wants you on the company's side when it's time to negotiate with the outside world.

The ultimate goal is to maximize your return. Maximizing your return in an employment agreement may mean more equity, more protection, a higher salary, a higher commission rate. On the back-end, maximizing your return in a separation agreement may mean more cash in your pocket, or accelerated vesting. But maximizing your return may mean other things, for example, not burning any bridges.

Ask yourself: "Do I maximize my return if I negotiate directly with the principal on the other side?"

My experience tells me: Yes, most of the time, you should negotiate the key business terms yourself.

Many times, I've sent the just-fired-entrepreneur or recently canned executive to negotiate directly with the devil who just fired him. I've been right there as shadow counsel (see below for more about shadow counsel), giving advice, ghost-writing the talking points, but not in the room.

In a friendly negotiation for employment, or alternatively, a tense but-lawyers-are-not-yet-involved back-end severance negotiation, the principals negotiating often go farther (in terms of maximizing your return), more quickly, more cheaply, and with less stress, than when lawyers are involved.

Too many lawyers don't know how to negotiate. They wind up slowing down, or messing up negotiations, rather than expediting them. In addition, if lawyers are negotiating directly, the decisionmaker on the other side might shift from a collaborative attitude to a let-the-lawyers-deal-with-this mentality.

You can, of course, directly negotiate with your lawyer by your side. Sometimes it's much more efficient for you and your lawyer to meet the employer's CEO or Board member with her lawyer, face-to-face, in a room, to negotiate the contract from top to bottom. The goal: to hit "print" and sign the agreement at meeting's end.

Sometimes, a good lawyer will be able to negotiate a better deal than you can yourself. Usually, there is something dysfunctional going on (e.g., sexual harassment, drunk boss, firing notice received via FedEx or text) that requires an attorney-to-attorney negotiation.

Additionally, there are other times where getting the deal done often requires lawyers to directly negotiate. Employment and equity negotiations during an acquisition come to mind.

Don't Negotiate with HR if You Can Avoid it

Don't negotiate with HR if you can help it. Go to the business decisionmaker who just offered you the job, or who just fired you, or who just offered you something else you want to negotiate.

If that person isn't the decisionmaker, then go to her boss, or boss' boss, whoever is the appropriate decisionmaker, with the power to grant your asks. Don't let HR insert itself between you and the business decision maker, if you can help it. Not on the front-end, and not on the back-end.

For the most part, HR isn't your friend. HR can't help you if a business executive doesn't want it to. Don't kid yourself otherwise.

On the back-end, basically HR's job is to smile a lot and tell you "no," to protect the corporation, to shield the executive team from you, to run interference, all as mellifluously as possible. This may be a bit harsh, but you get the idea. (Yes,

I've represented multiple high-powered HR executives over the years ... and helped them negotiate separation packages!)

How many times have I had a C-Suite executive tell me HR assured him that his employer never, ever gives what the C-Suite executive just asked for? Many times.

And how many times has that same C-Suite executive told me that HR is lying because, "I've given that to execs I fired?" Many times.

In over two decades of practice, I think that HR made the actual, ultimate decision in a sophisticated back-end separation negotiation, once, perhaps, twice. For your significant asks, HR invariably requires the approval of a business decisionmaker.

Negotiate directly with the decisionmaker, if you can!

What Airline Do You Fly?

"She's toxic," Sean's Irish brogue gave our conversation an international flair.

"What do the others on your team say?" I asked.

"Nobody can stand her. But the Board loves her."

Sean Joosta had come to America at 19 from County Kerry. With an Irish mother, Swedish father, and Peruvian wife, Sean speaks English, Irish, Swedish, Spanish, and passable Japanese on account of a three-year stint in Tokyo. Sean never went to college, but he's a spectacular salesman, and he's worked his way up the corporate ladder. At 43, he was Boabab, Inc.'s EVP of World Wide

Sales. Boabab is headquartered in Houston, but Sean works remotely most of the time from his home in Incline Village, Nevada.

"Why's that?" I asked.

"Because she's smarter than anyone else in the room. She's also the inventor. Plus, three of the Board members made money with her at her last company."

"Boabab's sales have been great until this year," Sean continued. "We beat the numbers every quarter for the last three years. But we plateaued this year. That's because there are no new products and none in the pipeline. I can't grow sales by 40% this year with no new products. No matter how much she micromanages. No matter how many times she threatens to fire me."

"Is she going to fire you?"

"I have no idea. But working for her is worse than a firing. The micromanaging, the threats, the insults, the pressure. I've killed myself for three years."

"Think about asking for a package."

"If I do that, she'll fire me."

"Then, will you get a package?"

"I don't know."

"Think about this," I said. "Get on her calendar. Fly down to Houston. Make sure you say, 'I'm not resigning' and 'I'm happy to continue working and building this company forever.' After that you can say, 'But if you don't want me here, then that's OK. Just offer me a professional separation agreement and I'll leave.'"

"I'll send her an email as soon as we're off the phone."

"Absolutely not! Fly down there, make your ask face-to-face. ... Can you get on her calendar?"

"Sure. But, I'm busy tomorrow and Wednesday. Maybe I'll just FaceTime her. I can't stand being in the same room with her."

"This is America. You can do what you want. But I urge you to fly down there and talk with her face-to-face. That's much better than FaceTime."

"When was the last time you went to visit the she-devil?"

"You're much more likely to get what you want if you make your ask in person. You know that. You're in sales."

Do it Face-to-Face

I don't care who you are. I don't care what your position is, or was. I don't care how badly you feel. If it's safe for you to do so, at all possible, and you're doing the negotiation, then negotiate face-to-face.

The studies are clear: You're more likely to get what you want if you make your ask face-to-face. It's harder for the other side to say, "no," when you're looking her in the eye.

Multiple times, at my behest, executives and entrepreneurs have taken coast-to-coast plane rides to make their face-to-face asks because the person(s) making the decisions worked 3,000 or so miles away. It doesn't always mean you'll achieve your negotiating goals, but the chances are higher that you will.

Don't Think About Telephone or Email or Text or Videoconferencing or Facetime

Not by videoconference. Not by Google Hangouts. Not by Facetime. Not by Zoom. Not by telephone, if you can avoid it.

Certainly not by email.

Not by text, nor by iMessage, nor by What's App.

Maximize your potential return. Make your ask in person.

Be Imaginative if Necessary

Be imaginative if you wind up in an unusual, atypical, or tough negotiation. Be entrepreneurial in your negotiations, in your asks and concessions. Know your goals, and the ways to get to the top of your personal mountain. This is the best way to have a chance at maximizing your return.

Remember: If it's legal, you can contract for it.

If it's legal and you have leverage, your imaginative asks might be achievable.

Who Cares if Your Employer Goes First?

Most employers like to "own" the documents. They want to go first. First to send you an offer letter or employment agreement. First to send you a change in control agreement. First to send you an equity agreement. First to send you an indemnification agreement. First to send you a separation agreement. Employers love to feel in control. They love to feel that they are dictating the negotiations.

Let them go first. Let them feel all those things. The employer going first is pretty much the natural order of almost all employer-employee negotiations.

Remember: It takes two to reach an agreement. If you have leverage – something your employer, would be employer or ex-employer desires – it really doesn't matter who goes first.

With a good marked up, revised agreement, you just went first. You told the other side what you want. It's all a matter of perspective. The key: Know what you want and how to express yourself.

If you have any ability to negotiate, then you may want an experienced lawyer to help you. A skilled lawyer will undoubtedly tell you that she can turn whatever agreement the company sends you into a pro-you document … if you're willing to negotiate.

Praveen and Henley

I cut Henley off. "Lose the emotion. Being emotional is going to hurt you."

I continued, "This negotiation is just like any other negotiation you've done. The only difference is that the widget here is the value of your labor. Treat yourself like a widget when you negotiate. You are trying to maximize your exit. Be assertive, but respectful, when you negotiate. Cold and calculating."

"When Praveen got the job as COO, he actually said to me, 'So now that I am COO, everyone's going to wash my feet. What are you going to do for me?'" Henley was angry. He was Chief Revenue Officer at a large public multinational.

Praveen had detested Henley for going on ten years, almost as long as the two had been employed (their start dates are a month apart). At a company picnic the summer of their first year on the job, Praveen was playing goalie in a pick-up soccer game. Henley beat him three or four times, celebrating each goal with a victory dance. Praveen was certain Henley celebrated to make him look bad, and had shunned Henley ever since. Over the past ten years, Henley and Praveen had worked their way up the corporate ladder, always in different parts of the organization, never reporting to each other. However, three months before, Praveen had been promoted to COO, with Henley as one of his reports.

"What did you say?" I asked Henley.

"I told him, 'I'm not going to do a damn thing for you. Go see Bob.'"

"Who's Bob?"

"His sycophant. Praveen says, 'You're a dog,' Bob barks; 'No you're a smaller dog,' Bob woofs; 'No, you're a cat,' Bob meows."

"So, what do I have to do again? I don't look like a widget."

"Look him in the eye," I responded. "Tell him that the separation agreement is not acceptable, and you expect a professional exit package. Be assertive, but respectful."

"Based on everything you told me, tell Praveen: two year's accelerated vesting, two years' severance, two years' COBRA. You're not going to get that, but it's a place to start. Make sure at the end to say that you have changes to the release that your lawyer will handle once you reach a deal on the key business terms. You want Praveen to know there will be smaller asks after you're done with the big picture issues."

"Do I have to do this?"

"Cold and calculating. Face-to-face. Just like negotiating for widgets."

"If I'm a widget, what does that make Praveen?"

Your Lawyer's Roles (If You Have a Lawyer)

Your Lawyer as Shadow Counsel

Do you tell your employer that you have a lawyer? That's a strategic decision. The goal: to maximize your return. If telling the other side that you have a lawyer maximizes the chances of your return, then tell your employer.

Think of it this way: If you're a CEO, how sharp will your Board think you are if you don't have a lawyer? Similarly, if you're a CFO, EVP, CMO, CTO ... someone on the executive team, consider whether your CEO might expect you to have a lawyer.

Whether you tell the other side that you have a lawyer is a very different issue than whether you retain a lawyer to help you. If you have a lot on the line – in any type of negotiation – the cheapest thing you may ever do is hire a lawyer. You might even convince your employer or ex-employer to pay for your lawyer (more about this later).

If you need help, hire a lawyer who knows what she's doing to be your shadow counsel. She'll advise you throughout the process, but behind the scenes. Your shadow counsel may work with you on your talking points, maybe draft your emails or texts. Hopefully, she'll provide sound advice, never appearing at the negotiating table until you and the life cycle of the negotiation are ready.

Your employer may know, even expect, that you have a lawyer. You undoubtedly know your employer is advised by an attorney (most employers have counsel). But keeping your shadow counsel in the shadows may help you optimize the results of your negotiations.

Your Lawyer Should Negotiate the Legalese

If you're entering into a protective offer letter or employment agreement, a mid-employment deal, or a back-end separation agreement, once you're done negotiating the key business terms (with your lawyer as shadow counsel), you'll probably want your lawyer involved.

You don't really want to be negotiating the definitions of "Cause" or "Good Reason," nor the other important "legalese" frequently featured in a protective employment agreement. That's not your bailiwick. Similarly, on the back-end, negotiating important carve-outs to the release and the like almost certainly isn't within your purview.

Out of the shadows, your lawyer appears to negotiate the legalese. Hopefully, she'll close your deal.

Blame Your Lawyer

Blame your lawyer if that's the way to maximize your return.

There are three I'm-blaming-my-attorney categories. Category #1: You blame your attorney for negotiating "too hard" for you. That's when you ask for the sky, the moon, and the stars. When your employer or would-be employer is offended, you point to your lawyer as quickly as possible and blame her for making over-the-top asks.

It's not as if your attorney makes outlandish asks without your approval. Your employer or would-be employer understands this. Nevertheless, attributing them to your "overzealous" lawyer, pooh-poohing her for being a lawyer, might advance your negotiations.

I'm guessing psychologists have a name for the phenomenon. All I know is that blaming-my-attorney Category #1 can sometimes be very effective. Multiple times over the years, I've told entrepreneur and executive clients, "blame it on me."

Category #2: You blame your lawyer for insisting on a must-have term or clause in your contract. As a result, you insist that the term is a deal breaker. The my-attorney-is-insisting-on-this-clause category is sometimes useful when your employer or prospective employer insists on a term that you find completely unacceptable. You may be able to achieve your goal while deflecting your employer's or would-be employer's anger on your obstinate adviser.

Category #3: You blame your lawyer for taking too long to review the offer letter your prospective employer sent you. This is the ol' my-lawyer-is-slammed explanation. Using this excuse may afford you more time to think (coldly and calculatingly) about your job offer.

But be careful when using the I'm-blaming-my-lawyer tactic. It could backfire if things go wrong and litigation or arbitration results because the other side might claim you've waived the attorney-client privilege as to your communications with your attorney. Once you voluntarily tell an employer, would-be employer or ex-employer what your lawyer said to you, the communication is no longer attorney-client privileged (because you voluntarily disclosed it). This means that in court the other side might be able to force you, or your lawyer, to testify about this and other confidential communications between you and your attorney.

Things to Remember

- Negotiate directly with the decisionmaker.
- Don't negotiate with HR, if at all possible.
- Negotiate face-to-face.
- Negotiate face-to-face.
- Negotiate face-to-face (getting the idea?).
- Be imaginative if your negotiation is unusual or difficult (if yours is a more "typical" negotiation, be creative if doing so breaks a logjam).
- It's no problem to let your employer go first. When you counter with a good revision, you just went first.
- Use your lawyer wisely in your negotiations.

8

The Professional Prenuptial Agreement

No Accelerated Vesting?

"You have to call this guy back. Mij referred him to you," Molly, my executive assistant said. She stood in the doorway. Molly has been with me so long that she knows which new potential clients get a call back right away.

"Do I have to? These other matters are driving me crazy."

"Yes, you have to. He said he's Mij's college buddy or something like that. He's got a big problem. If you don't call him back, Mij is going to stop lunching with you."

"He never pays for lunch anyway."

"At least he has lunch with you."

"OK... Who is this guy and what's his story?" I ask. Molly interviews all potential clients who call the office, and then tells me their situation. Molly can talk with anyone about anything. She's heard some real doozies over the years.

"His name is Sylvester Hunt. He is EVP of Operations at Reb-Larry. Reb-Larry is public. Sylvester says the company got a new CEO about four months ago when the prior CEO retired. The new CEO has been micromanaging since day one, and Sylvester's been pushing back. Yesterday, the CEO fired Sylvester. HR was in the room. They said they would give Sylvester a separation agreement in a few days. Sylvester wants help negotiating the separation agreement."

"Doesn't he have an employment agreement?"

"He said he has an offer letter from when he started ten years ago. He wasn't an EVP then. Sylvester says that the offer letter gives him two months' severance pay."

"Sylvester has stock worth $425,000 vesting at the end of each quarter for the next two years and he doesn't want to lose it."

"How much stock?"

"About $3.4 million in in-the-money stock options and RSUs in the next two years."

"He doesn't have accelerated vesting in the offer letter?"

"He says he doesn't. He says he only gets accelerated vesting if there is a change in control, and that's as a result of a change in control agreement all the execs received about a year-and-a-half ago."

"What should I do?"

"You're speaking with him at 3:00 pm today."

Your Goals & Desires

You Need Protection!

If you don't mind getting dumped out on the street with nothing but your resume, that's OK by me. In that case, you don't really need protection.

But if you want a soft landing as you get booted, or maybe a lucrative landing, or simply to walk away with something additional for your hard work, then protecting yourself in your employment agreement or offer letter is the answer.

Why else do you need protection? Because things aren't always the way they seem! That's true in life. And it could certainly be true at your new job. You may have been conned, lied to, sold a bill of goods during your job interviews. Only after taking the job might you realize you've just hired on to a sh*t show.

Haven't you ever talked up something so that it seemed better than it really was? Don't you think there are employers out there who may do the same?

What's another reason you might need protection? Because things that go well early on sometimes go bad down the road. Bosses come and go. Companies sell. Companies merge. Companies reorganize. Companies lay off employees. Companies go bankrupt.

You could be a star one minute, a goat the next, and unwanted baggage at the end. Protect yourself and you don't need to worry.

Professional Prenuptial Agreement v. Golden Parachute – It's All a Matter of Perspective

Best is to protect yourself and negotiate your separation agreement before you begin work. That's the professional prenuptial agreement I've been writing about. If your employer fires you, you walk away with whatever you negotiated, the more the better.

But a third party might look at you and think how privileged you are … because to him or her it seems like you have a golden parachute, a golden parachute that ensures a soft (or super soft) landing on firing.

Your golden parachute can lead to jealousy, even hatred because, let's face it, most Americans don't have golden parachutes. Most Americans who are fired, find themselves on the street, with only unemployment insurance to protect them (if they qualify for unemployment insurance).

There was substantial pushback a number of years ago against big severance agreements when companies change hands, for example when your employer is sold to another company. Congress reacted with a law. Now there's an extra parachute payment tax of 20% for those who receive "too much" after a merger. Congress defined "too much" as more than three times average compensation over the past five years.

To you it's a protective prenuptial employment agreement or well-negotiated separation agreement. To others it's a golden parachute. To Congress, it might be an excessive parachute payment. It's one and the same and depends on your perspective.

0-2

To: Shauna Caitlen Solicitor
From: Lourdes Sol
Date: 18 September @ 3:43
Re: One More Time

Dear Shauna:

I know you told me I should take some time off after my last disaster, but I couldn't resist talking with Sidnee about the new COO opportunity at Porto Importante. Will you be available this weekend to look at my offer letter when it comes in? They said they will email it to me by 5 pm Friday.

I know. I know. I know. I can hear you saying, "Don't just accept the first opportunity you come across. Do your personal due diligence. Make sure the next place is the right place for you. No more calamities Lourdes!"

Like I told you I've got one more equity play in me. If that doesn't work, then I'm going straight for the cash. No failed equity deals after 40 is my motto!

You know I've been so close twice already. I really should have become financially independent on the first rodeo – you wrote me such a great contract. It's really too bad the stock plummeted three weeks before the lock-up was lifted, and I got the big equity donut.

And the management carve out agreement you negotiated for me at my last job was so great. My B-School friends told me how good the deal was. Too bad the company sold below the first payment waterfall. I was sure it would go north of that.

It's not good to be 0-2, I know, but I'm going to try one more time, and hope you'll have time this weekend to help me negotiate a great contract again.

Third time's a charm!
Lourdes

Make Sure You Check Out Your Would-Be Employer

Would you buy a car without test driving it? Would you propose marriage without going on at least a few dates?

Then why in the world would you join a new employer without checking out your would-be employer as much as possible before joining? And I mean as much as possible.

Many times, clients have called me to tell me the job they just took isn't anything like it was described.

Many times, clients have called to tell me how much they left on the table to join a new employer, only to discover that the job interviewers had misled them, and there is little of worth (not much long-term value) at the new employer.

The largest companies are not immune, I can assure you. The highest levels are not immune either. Multiple C-Suite executives have called over the years perplexed that the main product of the company they just hired on to run doesn't work the way it is supposed to work.

Of course, if your job interviewer is a convincing liar and chooses to lie, you may be defrauded. It's hard to ferret out an excellent liar.

But most people don't commit fraud. They just stretch the truth, or sometimes hope the truth is the way they say it is.

Trying hard to figure out "what's really going on" at your would-be employer and with your future boss is doing your "personal due diligence."

One of the best ways to check out your prospective employer is to take a former executive of the company out for drink or dinner and ask what it's really like working there.

If you want to find out about your next boss, try to speak with someone who once worked with the guy. That someone might tell you the truth, or hopefully, at least leave you with thoughts for you to interpret. It's certainly worth a try.

If you're joining a public company, then a lot of information is only an internet search away. Public companies are required to file disclosures with the SEC, revealing significant details about their financials and employment deals and policies.

Among other things, the employment agreements of a number of executives will be there for you to read. Read them, especially if you're hiring on as a C-Suite executive.

If you're joining as CEO or CFO, you'll be able to see the prior CEO's and CFO's employment agreement – wouldn't it be nice to know what they received and how Cause and Good Reason were defined (assuming they have those clauses)?

If you're joining as another of the company's C-Suite officers, not only might the employment agreements be useful, but so too might other of your prospective employer's company-wide or executive-wide plans, such as disclosed long-term incentive plans, retirement plans and severance plans.

None of this is to say that you might not choose to hire on to a terrible employer. You might decide to do so. The money may be too good. The equity special. The ability to use something terrible as a stepping stone to better advance your career. There are many reasons to hire on to the dreadful employer. But if you're going to do so, you should do so coldly and calculatingly, with eyes wide open. And protect yourself with a professional prenuptial agreement, if possible.

Don't Get Cheated Out of Equity

If you're *not* familiar with the concepts discussed below, then read this section over and over again until you truly understand. Too many have been screwed by too few because they didn't understand their equity.

I don't care whether you are a newbie out of college, are a newly minted MBA, or have been paid millions in the past to run a division of a Fortune 500 company. None of these accomplishments guarantees you understand equity.

Beware: If you're equity-uneducated, you expose yourself to equity rip-offs, or equity misunderstandings, depending on your perspective.

What Percentage of Your Employer Do You Own?

You've just been offered an option for 1,000,000 shares of Beach International's common stock! 1,000,000 shares! Isn't that fantastic?!

With 1,000,000 shares vesting over four years, you'll have them all in just four years. And if you receive 100% accelerated vesting if you are fired without Cause or resign for Good Reason, you've locked in those million shares. Locked them in!

So, what???

That you're receiving one million shares of Beach International means nothing, without more context.

1,000,000 shares may be a lot of shares or a dearth of shares, depending on a number of factors, including the total number of shares outstanding. In other words, the total number of shares you own, or you will receive the right to own via an equity award, is totally meaningless. What matters is how much of (the percentage of) the fully diluted equity of the company the total number of shares represent.

Let's look more closely at the fully protected option for the 1,000,000 shares of stock in Beach International you were just offered. If Beach International has 1,000,000,000 shares of stock issued and outstanding, how much of the company does your 1,000,000 shares represent? Answer: 0.10%, in other words one-tenth of one percent.

Let's say Beach International's value is $100,000,000 and let's say all of Beach International's shares are the same in all respects. What is the value of your 0.10%? Answer: $100,000. Not chump change, for sure. But you can't retire on it.

Now let's say Beach International's fully diluted capital is 5,000,000 shares. How much of Beach International do your 1,000,000 fully protected option shares represent? Answer: 20%. If Beach International is still valued at $100,000,000, what is the value of your 20%? Answer: $20,000,000. You can retire on that.

At public companies, it's easy to tell the value of your shares. You should be able to check the price every minute or so from your computer if you want to.

You can figure out the percentage of a private company you own (or will own), by getting ahold of the company's capitalization table, "cap table" for short.

Failing the cap table (many employers don't like to divulge their cap tables), you should demand a copy (or buy one yourself) of your employer's amended and restated certificate of incorporation (or whatever the state where your employer is incorporated calls this document). The amended and restated certificate of incorporation (this is what it's called in Delaware) sets out the company's capitalization structure and its overhang (see below).

If your employer won't provide a cap table, make sure it represents to you in your employment agreement the percentage of fully diluted capital of the company, on an as converted to common stock basis, the number of shares you will be receiving represent.

Yes, I know, "the percentage of the fully diluted capital of the company on an as converted to common stock basis" is a mouthful. Write the phrase down so you don't forget it.

If your employer lies to you about the fully diluted capital your shares represent, that might be securities fraud. When the misrepresentation is *in writing* in your employment agreement, it will be hard for your employer to say it never made the representation. Most employers don't want to commit securities fraud.

Also, very important: remember that your ownership percentage doesn't mean very much until you find out your employer's valuation. 20% of $0 is $0. 20% of $100,000,000 is $20,000,000.

Not Good Enough

"It's not enough," CEO Aarav Reyanish shrieked across cyberspace at banker Aldrich Bronwyn during the late-night Zoom meeting.

"Lucky for the banker, he's in Boston," EVP of Engineering Zana Dariush, thought to himself. Zana was not so lucky. He and Namar Hacohen, EVP of World Wide Sales, sat next to Aarav in the company's Goa Conference Room. Zana was sure the conference room walls weren't doing their job.

"I beg to differ," Aldrich replied, the Bostonian's gigantic face looming from the screen on the Goa conference room wall. "Two hundred fifty million dollars is a commercially reasonable offer for the company. The multiple is right in the range we discussed."

"He's probably right," Zana thought, "but that doesn't mean he's going to get anywhere with Aarav." Zana said nothing.

"I don't care," Aarav screamed. "Two hundred fifty million is not good enough. I told you that before. I'm telling you that now. I'm not going to the Board with that offer."

"No more texts, no more emails, no more calls, no more Zoom meetings. Not until you have a better offer in hand," Aarav shouted at Aldrich as he terminated the meeting.

"Thank god," Zana thought.

As Aarav stormed out of the conference room, Zana looked over at Namar. Namar stared down at the table, lips pursed. "He has no idea what's going on," Zana thought.

"He's probably calculating that his two percent of two hundred fifty million dollars means five million dollars in his pocket."

When Namar looked up at him, Zana said, "So much for that condo you were looking at. Two hundred fifty million isn't going to buy any of us a cup of coffee."

"You get what I'm talking about, don't you?" Zana was sure he didn't. "We can't sell at two-fifty or below."

"I don't understand," Namar replied. "You own 20% of the company. That's fifty million dollars if we sell for two hundred fifty million. Aarav owns 30%, that's seventy-five million dollars. Why wouldn't we sell the company?"

"Sales guys, they never pay attention to details," Zana thought.

"Nobody here will get anything if the company is sold for two hundred fifty million because our liquidation preferences are two hundred fifty million," Zana said. "The preferred stockholders invested one hundred twenty-five million and they have a 2X liquidation preference, which means they get back twice their investment before anyone else gets anything."

"What are you talking about?" Namar asked.

"Liquidation preferences."

"What are liquidation preferences?"

"Liquidation preferences are the rights that the investors received when they invested. The investors put one hundred twenty-five million into this company, and when they invested the company agreed that the first two hundred fifty million of our sales price will be paid to the investors before anyone else gets anything."

"You're kidding me," Namar was aghast. "Why didn't you tell me?"

"There was nothing to tell. It's all in the corporate documents," Zana replied.

Does Your Employer Have Liquidation Preferences?

If you care about the value of your equity and your employer is a private company, then you need to know whether your employer has liquidation preferences, and if so, how bad they are. If you don't know your private employer's liquidation preferences, then you have a *huge hole* in your understanding. "Liquidation preferences" are also known as the company's "overhang."

Because of liquidation preferences, you might own 80% of a company about to be sold for $200,000,000, yet your shares are worthless.

Don't despair: if the share certificates are paper (rather than electronic), you should be able to wallpaper your room with them.

Not every company has liquidation preferences, but if yours does, you might not be receiving what you think you are receiving unless you know what those preferences are.

A company with preferred stock typically gives liquidation preferences to the holders of the preferred stock. If your employer has received investment from venture capital, private equity or other sophisticated investors, it's a pretty good bet that the investors hold preferred stock and your employer has an overhang (its investors have liquidation preferences).

Your employer's overhang determines how much of your employer's sales price (when your employer is acquired) is paid to the preferred stockholders before any dollars are paid to you and the other common stockholders. You and the company's other employees almost surely own (or have options or RSUs for) your employer's common stock. Common stock is typically last in line to receive.

When someone talks about a 1X liquidation preference on a $50 million investment, she is telling you the investors will receive the first $50 million of your employer's sales price before you, a common stockholder, receive anything.

She is also probably telling you (you gotta read the docs to be sure!) that if the preferred stock converts to common stock (and receives a distribution as a common stockholder rather than preferred stockholder) the preferred stock will take equally with you, the common stockholder. In other words, if the preferred don't convert, the preferred receive the return of their $50 million investment and nothing more. But if the preferred convert, then the preferred will receive the same amount of the sales price per share as you do.

On the other hand, when that same someone tells you the investors have a double participating preferred preference on a $50 million investment, she is probably telling you (but you gotta read the docs!) that the preferred stockholders will receive the first $100,000,000 of your employer's sales price (receiving a return of double the $50 million invested), and after that, will receive the same amount of money per their share as you and the other common stockholders receive for your common stock (that's the participating part of the double participating preferred). Thus, if your employer sells for $100,000,000, you, as a common stockholder, receive $0 for your stock.

Do you see how important the overhang is? Do you see how important the characteristics and size of the liquidation preferences are? If not, re-read what you just read. It can be dense and may take a while to get it.

If your prospective employer doesn't provide the liquidation preference information you need, and it's a Delaware corporation, then get a copy of its most current amended and restated certificate of incorporation. All the preferences will be in the document (although it's probably really difficult to read). The certificate is public. You can order a copy from Delaware's Secretary of State. If your prospective employer is incorporated somewhere else, then read whatever that somewhere else calls its certificate of incorporation.

By the way, there's a number of ways to protect yourself against a bad overhang. You could go work somewhere else. Then you wouldn't have to worry about the overhang (just make sure the somewhere else doesn't have the same or a worse issue).

If you have leverage and are joining at the C-Suite level, you might be able to negotiate for a management carve-out agreement, guaranteeing you some amount of the sales price of your employer even if your equity is worthless (see two chapters ago for more on management carve-out agreements).

Or, you might be able to negotiate additional cash compensation to make up for equity you expect to be worthless.

Will You Be Diluted and By How Much?

If you're considering joining a start-up (or even a larger private company) that needs to raise investment capital (needs additional funding), you need to answer the following question: What percentage of the fully diluted capital of my employer will my equity represent after the dilution resulting from future investments (fundraising)? It may not do you any good to own 10% of a company today, if next month, your 10% drops to 1% because of an intervening financing.

A *reverse* stock split sometimes portends future or imminent dilution. A reverse stock split occurs when you wind up with 1 share of stock for some greater number of shares of stock you held before the split. Take for example the *reverse* 400 to 1 stock split. You wind up with 1 share of stock for every 400 shares of stock you held before the reverse split. By the way, you wouldn't be the first person to suffer a 400 to 1 reverse stock split!

A reverse split, itself, does not affect the percentage of your employer that you own because the reverse split will hit every shareholder the same way. However, reverse stocks splits sometimes signal dilution. The reverse split may be taking place in advance of or in connection with a dilutive equity financing or other dilutive financial event (such as a recap, short for recapitalization).

If you expect future dilution, ask yourself what, if anything, you want to do about it?

One strategy is to negotiate for more stock up front to cover future expected dilution. Another strategy is to negotiate for an additional equity grant after the dilution to cover the dilution. A third strategy is to wait and see what happens with the financing of your prospective employer before joining up.

Powerless

Jeff and Cain had been living and breathing DenaliOne for months, and they were ecstatic. Rursus Venture Partners had just agreed to invest $5 million into DenaliOne for 40% of the company and two of the five seats on DenaliOne's board of directors. Rursus would receive Series A preferred stock.

Jeff and Cain had met at college years before. Jeff was erudite and scholarly. He loved nothing more than a long walk in the woods with his wife, Flourish, or an even longer paddle out on the lake near where they lived. Cain was a hard charger, who cherished a great game of poker. The two were proof that opposites attract. Cain was best man at Jeff's wedding, and Jeff was the godfather of Cain's first child.

Jeff owned 80% of DenaliOne's common stock and Cain 20%. That's because the idea for the company was Jeff's, he had worked on DenaliOne for a year before Cain became involved, and he had invested $100,000 of his own money into the company, compared to Cain's $5,000. But Jeff and Cain always considered themselves co-founders.

Jeff and Cain couldn't wait to get Rursus' $5 million in the bank because now they could hire another ten employees. They just knew DenaliOne was a sure thing.

The two founders read every word in the mountain of financing documents DenaliOne's lawyers gave them, and then signed them with a smile.

The voting rights agreement between Jeff, Cain and Rursus obligated all shareholders to vote two seats on DenaliOne's board of directors to anyone Rursus designated, and three seats on DenaliOne's Board to anyone designated by a majority of the common stockholders employed by DenaliOne. At the close of the financing, Jeff, Flourish, Cain, and Rursus' two lead partners made up DenaliOne's Board.

Over the next seven months, DenaliOne grew, but not as fast as Rursus had hoped. Cain too was getting frustrated at the company's "slow" progress and his friend's management style, which he felt was too deliberate.

Then came the epiphany! Looking into the mirror one day, Cain realized the man staring back at him was the man to take DenaliOne to the next level.

At the Board meeting five days later, DenaliOne's Board voted 3-2 to fire Jeff, with immediate effect. The Board then voted 3-2 to appoint Cain Interim CEO until the Board could do a CEO search.

Jeff couldn't believe it. There had been no notice. No one had ever complained. And the best man at his wedding had voted to fire him. Jeff felt like he'd been shot in an ambush. Flourish was livid.

"Sorry buddy," Cain said to Jeff as the two left the Board meeting. "Rursus has been upset with the slow growth of DenaliOne for months, and I'm going to make this place fly. I'm going to make you super rich and me pretty rich. You still own 80% of the common stock."

Jeff was too hurt to say anything.

Jeff knew that he owned 80% of DenaliOne's common stock and figured he could take back control of DenaliOne by removing Cain and voting another friend onto the company's Board. The next morning, Jeff called a lawyer for advice on how best to proceed.

Jeff, Flourish, and the lawyer met two days later, after the lawyer had reviewed all of DenaliOne's corporate and financing documents.

"Unfortunately, there's a gotcha in the documents you signed," the lawyer began. "The voting rights agreement only gives you the right to vote three Board members onto DenaliOne's Board if you are currently employed by DenaliOne, which you are not. The only common stockholder with any power now, the right to vote three members to DenaliOne's Board, is Cain, even though he owns only 20% of DenaliOne's common stock."

Jeff didn't know what to say.

Don't Be Neutered by Your Company's Governance and Financing Documents

If you care about who controls your company and under what circumstances they control it, then you must read and understand every implication of every one of your employer's corporate governance and financing documents. All of them!

They're long. And they're boring. And they're difficult to understand. And they're full of legalese. But if you really want to know, you must read them all (or ask a lawyer or other trusted advisor to read them for you) and understand them.

Never, ever, sign a voting agreement, investor rights agreement, or any other agreement for that matter, unless you understand every word in the document.

There are big law firms out there who will do anything to satisfy their *repeat player* (meaning they give a lot of lucrative business to the law firm) private equity and venture capital investors and screw you the founder, or you the C-Suite executive with the legalese in the corporate documents they prepare.

And unfortunately, you may miss, or, because you've never been screwed before, not understand, the power underlying the neutering clauses. Make sure you know exactly what you are signing.

Coldly and Calculatingly Consider Everything

Maybe that job offer just feels right. Maybe you really think it will work out. Maybe....

I'm not opposed to you choosing your employer by gut feeling.

If you think you'll regret not taking that job later in life, then take the job. Life's too short. You can always quit when you're ready (unless your new employer makes the decision for you first).

But before taking the job on gut feeling, before taking the job because you believe you'll regret it if you don't, I urge you to carefully consider all the issues, coldly and calculatingly. Even if you ultimately decide to throw cold and calculating to the wind.

You might discover that cold and calculating consideration changes your gut feeling, or changes what you believe, initially. But if it doesn't, then at least you'll join your new employer knowing some of the risks you face.

If you need someone to help you reflect on all the issues coldly and calculatingly, then consult that someone, whether that someone is a friend, trusted advisor, experienced businesswoman, lawyer or another. The goal: To know what you are getting into when you get into it.

Your Requests

No, you shouldn't request that a new employer grant you whatever unreasonable amount of equity you decide you want. Same thing with salary and other parts of your comp package.

I take that back. If you don't care about the job and don't care about being reasonable (and appearing reasonable), then demand whatever amount of equity, salary, commissions you want, no matter how unreasonable. Who cares if your demand encompasses the sun and the moon and the galaxy and the next galaxy? It doesn't really matter.

However, if you care, then do your best to determine the equity, salary and other compensation ranges that are stretches, and decide whether you'll demand the stretch.

There is more or less a market for the equity, salary, bonuses and other comp you should expect to receive from a prospective employer. The problem is that the rough more-or-less market depends on so many factors. Those factors are both personal to you and company-specific.

Personal to you factors include: the job you're taking, your leverage, and your experience. For example, if you have previously successfully taken three private software companies public, then you are likely to receive much more equity in a software company about to go public as compared to a first time CEO.

Company specific factors include the size and financial condition of the company (e.g., Series A round financed company, small failing public company, Fortune 500 company, etc.), where your would-be employer is headquartered (you might get more equity in Silicon Valley than Hells Canyon, but maybe not), whether VC or PE are involved (good luck getting quantity or protection with NY-based PE investors), and what the company does (does it make chips, big molecules, security software, etc.). Also, don't forget about whether the company will suffer significant dilution if the company is private.

How to get the information you need might be a problem. The easiest way is probably to hire one of the comp consultants described in an earlier chapter to provide you the data. Anybody can hire them, but it's usually not required, and they can be expensive.

If you're going into a public company, then start with its publicly filed documents. But to ferret out the proper market range you may need to ask quite a few people. Like people who work there. Like people who work at similar size competitors.

Like advisors, lawyers, old geezers who have been there and done that....

Be as prepared as you can. You know your future employer's initial offer is probably not its last offer.

Things to Remember:

- Protect yourself with a professional prenuptial employment agreement if at all possible.
- Make sure you do everything possible to check out your prospective employer before joining up.
- Don't get cheated out of equity in a private employer: Know the percentage of your employer that you own (not just the number of shares).
- Does your employer have liquidation preferences (overhang), and if so, how bad are the preferences? If the overhang is large, do you have a management carve out or similar agreement to counteract the overhang?
- Will your equity be diluted, under what potential circumstances, and by how much?
- Make sure you understand every word of every document you sign. If you don't, get someone to help you understand.
- Before you sign on with a new employer, coldly and calculatingly consider every issue, even if you decide to throw your cold and calculating thoughts to the wind.
- Do your best to make commercially reasonable comp and equity demands.

9

Key Terms for Your Professional Prenuptial Agreement

Your Offer Letter Sucks!

Mr. Ken Ottawa
1 Neverbeenthere Lane
Palo Alto, California

Re: Your Ricky, Inc. Offer Letter

Dear Ken:

Because we've known each other for so long, I won't mince words: Your Ricky, Inc. ("Ricky") offer letter sucks! Haven't you learned anything over the years?!

You should already know what I'm going to say in this letter because you are now a three-time, crappy-offer-letter recidivist. Nevertheless, I'll repeat what I've told you before, but this time I'm increasing your friendship dues to a pair of tickets to the next World Cup Finals, and no, I'm not going to the game with your brother: I can't stand watching soccer with savants who would rather eat an overpriced burger than see goals scored.

The salary and bonuses Ricky is offering you are below market. Unless this is a pure equity play – and you told me, it is not – you should negotiate for more cash and better bonuses.

As you should know by now, your offer letter *does not protect you* in *critical* ways that many entrepreneurs and senior executives demand, because they have leverage to demand protection (if you don't think you have leverage, see a shrink ... and send me a second pair of World Cup tickets for the referral).

Your Ricky offer letter sucks because:

- You have *no* protection (e.g., no severance, no guaranteed bonus, no COBRA premium payments, no accelerated vesting of your equity) if Ricky's Board of directors demotes or otherwise mistreats you during your employment, or terminates your employment, or imposes Owen as an Executive Chairman.
- You have *no* protection for your equity in the first year of employment. Ricky can fire you after 11½ months of employment and you won't receive even one share of vested stock. That's because your stock option has a 1-year cliff and you haven't protected against the cliff's downside.
- You have *no* protection in the event Ricky undergoes a corporate change in control. You *risk losing all unvested shares* subject to your stock option if a merger or sale occurs. That's because Ricky's Equity Incentive Plan allows

Ricky to terminate your option in the event of a merger or sale.

- You have *no* protection in the event Ricky has a significant overhang – meaning high liquidation preferences. You resisted me last time about this and almost got screwed – lucky for you I insisted on a management carve-out deal.
- You have *no* protection if you die or become disabled.

You know perfectly well that California companies have wide discretion to hire, fire, and reassign their at-will employees, including their CEOs!, and to change everyone's responsibilities and rates of pay whenever they want. An employee (and certainly a CEO) protects himself against employment termination, reassignment, a reduction in wages, and other mistreatment by negotiating for strong "termination without Cause" and "Good Reason to resign" clauses (Good Reason clauses are sometimes called, "constructive termination" or "involuntary termination" clauses). You have neither protective clause in your Ricky offer letter.

A "termination without Cause" clause may provide you severance, COBRA premium payments, continued rights to incentive compensation, accelerated vesting of equity, and an extended post-termination exercise period for stock options (as well as any other terms you negotiate) in the event Ricky terminates your employment for reasons that have nothing to do with you acting improperly. Don't screw up: Make sure to define "Cause" narrowly!

A "Good Reason" clause can provide the same benefits in the event Ricky materially reduces the value of your employment relationship, such as by reducing your job title, authority, responsibilities, salary, benefits, reporting relationship, office location, or otherwise mistreats you.

Think of it this way: If I were Chairman of the Board, I would assign you to the copy room. Without a Good Reason clause, you would, in my regime, be forced to quit without benefits, or, maybe given your personality, you would press a lot of "print" buttons in the following years. Make sure your "Good Reason" definition is broad (always keeping in mind Internal Revenue Code § 409A, which basically restricts the potential breadth of the definition).

I urge you to negotiate for cash compensation (push for 12–24 months), accelerated vesting of your equity (push for 100%) and an extended post-termination exercise period (push for the life of the option) if your employment is terminated by Ricky without Cause or by you for Good Reason.

I also urge you to negotiate for full vesting of your equity on the closing of a change in control.

Because you will be joining Ricky as its CEO and because you have been a CEO twice before, I believe you have leverage to negotiate a much stronger and more protective offer letter.

I could go on and on with all the stuff you need in your offer letter and otherwise (what about an indemnification agreement?!), but the things I describe above are so important I'll stop here and simply encourage you to negotiate big picture stuff first. You can tell the Ricky Board member who gave you the hunk of junk offer letter that you'll negotiate the big picture stuff first, and after that, your friend the lawyer will negotiate the legalese.

So Ken Ottawa, to get it through your thick skull, let me repeat: I urge you to negotiate for additional salary and benefits, and for severance payments, severance benefits, accelerated equity vesting, and an extended post-termination exercise period in the event your employment is terminated by Ricky without Cause, or by you for Good Reason at any time, and full vesting upon the closing of a change in control.

If this letter doesn't compute, I am going to increase your friendship dues another couple of World Cup tickets.

Sincerely,
August Remero

Key Clauses for Your Offer Letter or Employment Agreement

If you want to learn about all the parts of an employment agreement, the nitty gritty anatomic details, every clause that should be in your employment agreement and what it should say, then have a look at *Executive Employment Law*, or better yet, hire an experienced lawyer to advise you. I don't go through all the technical details here. Instead, I write about clauses that matter most of the time. *Your situation, however, may call for more or different clauses, so please remember that.*

You may start out with a long list of "must haves." Many entrepreneurs and executives do. If yours is really a must have, then OK, it's a must have, and not getting it is a deal breaker. I understand that.

But I bet that your end-of-the-line must have list will be a lot shorter than your initial one. It turns out that when entrepreneurs and executives focus, or when the negotiation goes on for a while, many "must haves" are not really "must haves." Rather, most are "really likes." Good to remember.

What Matters!

Your Position

Make sure your employment agreement spells out your job responsibilities as much as possible. There are two huge benefits to doing so. The first – the more you and your prospective employer know what to expect, the more likely you'll avoid problems in the future.

The second – setting out your responsibilities in writing may help you if you ever decide to trigger the Good Reason clause you hopefully negotiate into your employment agreement. For example, if one of your jobs includes overseeing the IT Department, your employer takes away that responsibility and your Good Reason clause says you may resign and leave with severance if your responsibilities are reduced, then you are better off if your employment agreement lists overseeing the IT department as one of your responsibilities.

If you're being hired as CEO, you don't need to spell out your responsibilities. You should simply say in your employment agreement that you're responsible for the day-to-day operations of the company, or something similar. If your employer balks at this, then there will probably be an "executive chairman of the board" looking over your shoulder. And if not an executive chairman, something else is going on, and you should find out what that is.

Your Base Salary

A select few entrepreneurs and execs are equity-play only.

For everyone else, cash compensation matters. It all starts with your base salary. Make sure you know your base salary, that it is acceptable, and when it will be paid.

Thinking About Moving Companies

"How much are you leaving on the table if you quit now?" I asked long-time client Nicky Yitzhak. Two hours before, Nicky had emailed me an offer letter and asked to speak. He'd been offered a Chief Operating Officer job at Micah-Julia, a growing social media company.

"$650,000," Nicky responded. "My last tranche of $550,000 in restricted stock is coming my way at the end of this year, plus I have a $100,000 retention bonus payable on December 31st as well."

"The offer letter you sent me doesn't say anything about the six-fifty. Think about asking Micah-Julia to make you whole with a $650,000 signing bonus, or if the company can't stomach that, how about a $300,000 signing bonus and $350,000 more in stock options or restricted stock?"

"I'm going to ask for a $650,000 signing bonus and see what they do. The $650,000 is pretty much guaranteed if

I stay where I am and work through the end of the year. So, let's see if they'll buy me out. If not, I can always stay put."

"What about your annual bonus?"

"What about it?"

"It's an important part of your comp isn't it?"

"You bet. It's 70% of my salary at target so at target that's $350,000."

"How long do you think it's going to take for you to get Micah-Julia moving in the direction you and the CEO want it to move in?

"It'll take me at least nine to eighteen months, maybe more before I can get revenue where it should be. I'm going to have to make a lot of operational changes."

"If that's the case, then I suggest that you negotiate for a guaranteed bonus for the first nine to eighteen months of your employment. If that's too long for Micah-Julia, negotiate a guaranteed bonus for at least the next six months, through the end of this year. Otherwise, you probably won't earn a bonus the rest of this year and maybe not next year either because you just told me that it's going to take you at least nine months to right the ship."

Commissions, Bonuses & More

Many receive some percentage of their cash comp in the form of a bonus, often paid at target as a certain percentage of their base salary. For example, an EVP may earn $400,000 per year with a 50% bonus at target, meaning the EVP will receive another $200,000 in bonus for the year if the EVP achieves her bonus metrics.

What triggers the payment of the bonus? That depends on your employer and what you negotiate. There are so many different types of bonuses and milestones. You can have a bonus that pays 100% on a certain revenue target or hiring goal or EBITDA achievement (EBITDA stands for "earnings before interest, taxes, depreciation and amortization" and may be used as a metric to assess your company's profitability). On the other hand, you can have a bonus that is 100% discretionary.

Whatever bonus you sign up for, know exactly what you're getting and when, as well as the risks of not receiving it. The more discretionary, the squishier the triggers for your bonus, all things being equal, the less you should count on receiving your bonus.

Here's a number of things to watch out for with performance-based bonuses:

- Does your employment agreement say you will (or shall) be participating in a bonus plan or that you are eligible to participate in the plan? They may be the same thing, but I prefer saying you will (or shall) be participating.
- Do you know what the bonus plan says? You should.
- Is any part of the first year or two of your bonus guaranteed? You may want an initial guarantee, especially if the place you're planning on joining is so messed up, you won't hit the ground running, or if you're coming in the middle of the bonus cycle and will not have time

to improve performance against metrics in the stub part of the cycle.

- If new metrics will be set every year, what happens if they aren't timely set, or not set at all? If this happens, you probably want your bonus guaranteed or Good Reason triggered.
- When will your bonus be paid, and are you required to be employed when the bonus is paid? You probably want a bonus paid within 75 days of the end of the bonus period and one that is payable regardless of whether or not you're employed on pay day.
- If your employment is terminated part way through the year, will you receive a prorated bonus as part of your severance package? You probably want at least a prorated bonus, although if you have leverage, you might be able to negotiate for a bonus payable at target.
- Is your bonus based on easily ascertainable management-based objectives, or is it completely discretionary, or perhaps a combination of both? With easily ascertainable metrics, you know exactly what you will receive when you hit the metrics.
- Must any part of your bonus be repaid (subject to clawback), and if so, under what conditions? Do you really want a repayment obligation? Probably not.

There are certainly other types of bonuses. The signing bonus is a famous one. Experienced entrepreneurs and executives sometimes negotiate for hundreds of thousands, sometimes even millions of dollars in signing bonuses, especially when they're leaving significant sums on the table with prior employers (in this case the signing bonus acts as a buy-out of the former employer's benefits).

If sales is your field, then you almost certainly want a great commission plan, hopefully uncapped. Like bonus plans, there are numerous types of commission plans.

Make sure your commission plan is crystal clear about what your commission is and what you have to sell or do to trigger payment of commissions. There have been many disputes over non-payment (or under-payment) of commissions. The more everything in your commission plan is clear and straightforward, the better off you probably are. Review the list above regarding bonus plans – those watch-out-fors apply to your commission plan as well.

Your Equity

If you play the equity game, your professional prenuptial agreement must describe the equity you receive and the protections you negotiate. Remember, with the equity play, you'll probably earn less in cash comp than you can earn in a similar company that doesn't offer you significant equity.

If you're lucky, there is no question that the equity play may lead to the most expensive house, unimaginable riches, retirement in your 20's or 30's. But the potential upside comes with big risk, mostly the risk that your equity will turn out to be worthless. Good to keep that in mind.

Your Long-Term Comp

If you work for a mature company, you may receive bonus and equity comp plans designed to incentivize you to stay put, sometimes known as "golden handcuffs." These comp structures make it very expensive for you to quit your employer. If you leave, you'll leave cash on the table.

These types of comp strategies take many forms and go by various names. Sometimes they are defined benefit pension plans. When you hit retirement age, a defined benefit pension plan guarantees you a payout in your retirement years.

One type of comp structure is called the Long-Term Incentive Plan, "LTIP" for short. An LTIP plan is typically a milestone-based plan that guarantees a payout in future years based on whatever milestones are set when the plan is established.

So, for example, an LTIP plan might pay $250,000 in three years, $250,000 in four years and $250,000 in five years if your employer's gross annual revenue exceeds $77.4 million for any two of the first three plan years and you are employed on the plan's payment dates.

If your company meets the metric in year two of the plan, would you be willing to leave before you collect your $750,000 in LTIP payments? How about if you are no longer happy or content (or are outright miserable!) on the job?

What about if your employer starts another LTIP plan two years from now that pays $300,000 five years hence, $300,000 six years hence and $300,000 seven years hence if certain metrics are met in the first three years of that LTIP plan and you are employed on the payment date?

If you find it hard to walk away from LTIP payouts, you're not alone. That's the whole idea from your employer's perspective. You were offered the LTIP to discourage you from leaving.

Are You Getting Any Perks?

Check out your prospective employer's perquisites. They may make you happy.

If you want special perks, make sure to include them in your employment agreement. For example, if your prospective employer's policy allows for business-class travel only on trans-Atlantic or trans-Pacific flights and your job is going to require heavy Seattle to Philadelphia travel, you might want to include a clause in your employment agreement allowing you to fly business class on cross-country flights. The same is true if you want your employer to pick up your home office expenses, car lease, monthly cell phone bill or something else.

§ 162(m)

If you work for a public company, § 162(m) of the U.S. tax code allows your employer to deduct as a business expense up to $1 million of your total compensation, assuming you're a "covered employee" as federal law defines "covered employee." Total comp includes your base salary, bonus, RSUs and stock options.

If you're going to negotiate for that type of comp, then you probably want to know whether your employer cares about the § 162(m) limit. By checking your would-be employer's public filings, you might be able to figure out what your predecessor (or other execs at your prospective employer) earned.

Note that the largest and most successful employers pay total comp north (and often well north) of $1 million. They just don't deduct the excess.

They Can Take Back Money They Already Paid Me?

"Yes, you could be required to pay back all of your bonus if you compete with your employer at any time in the five years after you receive your bonus," I responded to Cindy Burgess. Cindy had asked me to review a "Special Bonus Agreement" that her employer said she needed to sign by the end of the week.

"They can take back money they already paid me?" Cindy was surprised. "There must be a law against that. Are you sure?"

"Yes, I'm sure. You live and work in a state that allows your employer to claw back special compensation it pays you even if you've spent the money, providing you agree in writing to allow the money to be clawed back, or 'recovered,' as it's referred to in your Special Bonus Agreement."

"Your company can't claw back your base salary, but a special bonus like this, it can claw back, if you agree in writing. To make matters worse, the Special Bonus Agreement requires you to pay back the entire bonus, even though you probably will have paid taxes on it. You need to see your tax advisor about what you'll do if that happens."

"Is there any way out of this?"

"Yes, don't sign the agreement. Or negotiate for a different agreement with your employer. Or go work for another employer that doesn't have compensation programs like this tied to non-competition."

Watch Out for Clawbacks

Beware of clawbacks! Clawbacks seek to take back from you cash you already earned and spent, equity you already cashed out and benefits you already received.

Clawbacks come in multiple varieties, but there are a few recognizable types of clawbacks out there.

One type of clawback is required by law. The federal Sarbanes Oxley Act established a required clawback on CEOs and CFOs of public companies in situations where their companies are required to tell the public that their financials are misstated, and thereafter, restate income (restating income is a fancy phrase for telling the public what a company's income should have been had it gotten the numbers right in the first place).

Employer clawback policies differ, so read them and understand them before hiring on to be an executive in a company with a clawback policy. You might also consider choosing one company over another based on its clawback policy. One of the most well-known clawback actions: In 2017, Wells Fargo clawed back more than $100,000,000 from two of its former executives.

It's one thing to have a clawback based on metrics that are defined and easily understood. For example, a clawback policy that requires you to return 100% of your bonuses if you or your team report revenue figures that force the company to restate income is an easy metric. Either your employer restates income (which it surely does not want to do) or it doesn't. Either you or your team is responsible for reporting the bad numbers (if you run sales, you or your team will probably be responsible) or you're not. Of course, there might be disputes about whether you or your team is responsible, but probably not so many.

On the other hand, it's quite another ball of wax if the clawback policy allows your employer to clawback 100% of your earned bonuses because you acted in a way the board of directors believes is detrimental to the best interest of your employer. The discretionary clawback puts you at risk both for forfeiture of earned compensation because a majority of the Board does not like you, as well as a potential victim of a hardball exit negotiation or renegotiation as a superior who doesn't like you presses the possibility of a clawback to steal back cash, equity and benefits you already pocketed.

Another type of clawback includes those that appear in compensation, bonus, deferred compensation or other contracts that require you, as a matter of contract, to pay back benefits under certain circumstances. One of those circumstances is you competing with your ex-employer. What do you think you will do if you receive a $500,000 bonus, which your employer may clawback anytime in the next five years if you compete?

Clawbacks triggered if you compete are unenforceable in some places, but totally valid in others. They are also sometimes used to chill your conduct even though they're illegal. Are you going to risk your employer suing you for the $500,000 even though you'll probably win?

One other thing to look out for with all clawbacks is whether you're required to pay the money back in the gross amount you received or the after tax in-your-pocket amount. If the former, that could really hurt.

They Cheat Me, But I Do OK

"$500,000 a year base; target bonus at 100% of salary; 800,000 shares over four years, 25% cliff vesting every year; they even have layered LTIP Plans. This is a great deal! I'm going to take it!" Nza Cicavek gushed.

Now 57, Nza is a CEO with repeat successes under her belt. The problem: about half the time Nza is mistreated by shady characters, often from New York, who would shoot their mothers for an advantage in a deal.

"So why are you calling me, Nza?"

"You know why! Years ago, I promised you're going to review every contract before I sign."

"The last time I reviewed a contract for you, you paid me good money ... and didn't listen to a word I said."

"And look what happened! I got cheated out of $4 million. But I still made three million when the deal closed. Not too shabby an upside for two-and-a-half years of work."

"And the deal before that I made $2 million on exit even though if I had listened to you, I would have made much more. I agree that wasn't as good a deal because it took almost five years."

"So, tell me how stupid I'm being this time," Nza asked.

"Did they offer you any severance pay?"

"3 months base salary if I'm terminated without Cause."

"That's not good for someone as successful as you. You should demand at least a year, and also payment of your full bonus. Whatever sleazebags you're doing a deal with this time will pay more. I'm positive."

"I thought you never guarantee anything, Mr. Lawyer."

"I don't. But if I went to Vegas, I would give long odds that they'll give you a better separation package if you demand it.... You haven't started working there yet, have you?"

"Not this time."

"You should also have a Good Reason to resign clause in your employment agreement, you know that."

"I know. I know."

"Is your equity protected in any way?

"I'm calling you so you can tell me how stupid I am. No."

"If you don't demand protection, you're selling yourself short. They will give you some."

"What do 800,000 shares mean?" I continued.

"The company is public and it's trading around $3.50 a share currently. The private equity investors own more than 50% of the company though."

"How protected are your shares?"

"I know. I know."

"So, you're telling me that if they fire you 364 days into your job, you get zero? And if they fire you when you've been on the job for 729 days, wait a minute, year after next is a leap year, for 730 days, you'll receive only 200,000 shares of stock and lose the remaining 600,000?"

"I guess so."

"What happens if there's a change in control?"

"I don't know."

"What do you mean you don't know?"

"I'm sorry. I forgot to ask."

"Don't be sorry for me. Be sorry for yourself."

"How do the LTIPs work?" I asked.

"The first LTIP is $5 million payable in four years based on a revenue, EBITDA, market share formula."

"If you hit the formula's metrics in year two and get fired in year three, what happens?"

"I don't know. I haven't read the plan."

"What do you want to do about all this?"

"I want you to give me advice about everything. Once I get your advice, I'll decide whether I'm going to ignore you this time."

Are You Convinced Yet?

Are you convinced yet that you require a professional prenuptial agreement? If so, read on:

Your Separation Package

You want severance if your employer fires you, don't you? You want severance if your employer mistreats you, say makes you work cutting the grass when you should be running the company, don't you?

How about 6 months of pay and pro-rated bonus plus 6 months of paid COBRA premiums? How about 12 months of pay and your bonus at target plus 12 months of COBRA? How about ....?

The first part of negotiating a separation package in your professional prenuptial agreement is determining how much comp and how many benefits you'll receive on exit. Generally speaking, there are commercially reasonable ranges, but those ranges depend on many things, including your seniority, whether your would-be employer is public or private, your prospective employer's industry, and so forth.

If you have leverage, definitely negotiate separation benefits into your employment agreement. That's the essence of the professional prenuptial agreement. I leave you to figure out the size of your exit package – you may want to consult an experienced professional to assist you.

The second part of negotiating a professional prenuptial agreement is determining the triggers (and sub-triggers) that result in separation benefits. If you don't do anything, but are mistreated or forced out anyway, you should receive separation benefits.

One trigger for receiving severance benefits is almost always, termination of employment by your employer without "Cause," sometimes known as "Involuntary Termination."

The other trigger you should negotiate into your contract is termination of employment by you for "Good Reason," sometimes known as a "Constructive Quit" or even, "Involuntary Termination." Some contracts combine the concepts into "Good Leaver" and "Bad Leaver" employment terminations.

You should negotiate as narrow a definition of "Cause" as you can. If you don't, your employer may be able to invent lots of reasons to fire you for Cause. If you're able to negotiate the following, you're golden: "For purpose of this employment agreement, 'Cause' means only your conviction of a felony crime of moral turpitude." Only one person I know negotiated a clause this narrow, so it's not likely such a narrow clause is in your future.

You should probably be happy with something like the following: "'Cause' means only your: (i) intentional, significant, and recurring failure to respond to a legal and sensible instruction from the board of directors; (ii) intentional, significant, and recurring gross neglect of your duties which causes material and measurable economic harm to the company, or (iii) conviction of a felony crime of moral turpitude." When you add a notice and cure period before you can be canned for

(i) and (ii), there's little chance an employer will be able to fire you except for the most egregious wrongs.

On the other hand, your employer wants two killer (anti-employee) triggers included in its dream "Cause" definition. One says something like, "'Cause' means (a) your inability to perform under your employment agreement." The other says something like, "'Cause' means your breach of any agreement between you and the company...."

Do you see how easy it is to terminate your employment for Cause under these two employer-dream definitions? Your employer could easily present you with a series of unattainable goals, and after you fail to work miracles, fire you for "failure to work miracles, as required."

The definition of "Good Reason" is also critical because you should protect yourself, if possible, in case you're mistreated. If your employer reduces your salary or your target bonus or your benefit package, or requires you to move far from your home, or demotes you, you want to be able to give the employer notice, and if your employer does not correct, then walk out the door with your separation package.

Defining "Good Reason" is trickier than defining "Cause" because of the morass that is Internal Revenue Code § 409A and its 397 pages of implementing regulations, not to mention follow-on IRS guidance. The tricky part is defining "Good Reason" in a way that does not upset the IRS (as mentioned earlier, § 409A's rules essentially restrict the potential breadth of the definition). Also, a "Good Reason" clause should almost always have notice, cure, departure, and timing requirements.

Because of this, you should retain a lawyer to help you with your definition of Good Reason.

By the way, you should negotiate for protection whether or not your employer undergoes a change in control (sale, merger, etc.). If you do not have single trigger protection on termination of employment, then you'll receive nothing if your employment is terminated without Cause by your employer or by you for Good Reason before a change in control. Why would you agree to that? Many do. But why would you?

I Want to Diversify

"What's the best way to get myself fired?" Cactus Subi was a long-time client, going back maybe fifteen years.

"Guess what?" I responded.

"What?"

"You don't see the use in communicating with me when things are going good." It was my joke to myself. Cactus was the number two guy over at QAK Security, Inc. He had started as a coder and worked his way up from there. About ten years before, while times were good, I had asked Cactus to dinner. He had declined telling me, "I don't see the use in that."

"What's the problem this time?" I asked.

"My CEO and his two favorite Board members are a three-headed hydra. They're monsters. I can't stand dealing with them anymore," Cactus replied.

"And thanks to you I don't have to! I've been here three years so if they fire me now, the rest of my unvested stock all accelerates, and best of all, I have five years to decide whether to exercise my fully vested stock option! Plus, I get six months' severance."

"I'm going to go somewhere else and diversify," Cactus explained. "If this company goes public, I'm rich."

"But there's no reason to have all your eggs in one hydra's basket. I love you man!"

"If I remember correctly," I responded, "you get five years after the last day of your employment to exercise your option regardless of why your employment terminates."

"But not all my stock. I need to get fired for that. You know I'm a greedy capitalist. I want it all!"

"So how do you recommend I go about getting myself fired so I can collect on that jewel you negotiated for me?

Clauses That'll Help You Protect Your Equity

Don't let anyone steal back your stock.

If your employment is terminated without Cause by your employer or for Good Reason by you, then you want:

- Accelerated vesting of your equity;
- An extended post-termination exercise period (for options);
- No forfeiture clauses; and
- Probably, although not always, no forced repurchase clauses (best is you have a right to require your employer

to repurchase your shares – a "put" option – but your employer has no right to require you to sell them).

Accelerated vesting means the vesting of your equity accelerates by some amount when you're fired without Cause or resign for Good Reason.

The first thing you must do is defeat the vesting cliff. The cliff is the date when the option vests and usually indicates there's been no vesting before that time (or no vesting since the last cliff). For example, if your stock options or RSUs vest over four-years, with a one-year cliff, and monthly vesting thereafter, and you're fired in the middle of your 11th month of employment, you receive no equity because you didn't get past the cliff. But if the vesting of your equity accelerates by one year, you will always beat the cliff.

The second thing you should do is negotiate for accelerated vesting beyond the cliff. If you have leverage, say you are a repeat CEO, then you might be able to negotiate for 100% acceleration of all unvested equity if you're fired without Cause or leave for Good Reason. With less leverage, you may have to settle for six months or one year of accelerated vesting.

You want the acceleration clause to say that you will receive that number of vested shares as you would have received had you worked to the date that is as many days into the future as you negotiated for acceleration. So, with one year accelerated vesting, as an example, if you're fired after six months for no reason, your accelerated vesting clause should be written so you vest in 18 months of shares, or 18/48ths if you are on a four-year vesting schedule, even if you have a cliff. If your contract just says you receive one year of accelerated vesting, in the same situation, you would receive 12/48th of the shares. Pay attention to this.

Beware of forfeiture clauses. Many option agreements say that you forfeit everything, even your vested shares, if your employer fires you for Cause. Many an employer will have an incentive to fire you for Cause if you agree to a forfeiture clause like this. Get rid of all forfeiture clauses. Period!

Beware too of the forced repurchase clause. Even if the forced repurchase of your vested equity is at a fair market price (i) you will be giving away the potential exit premium, the amount the stock might rise simply because of an exit, and (ii) in some cases, your contract may define "fair market value" in a sleazy way (let's say book value is used, or a value "as determined by the board of directors in their sole discretion"). These provisions could cost you a fortune.

If you want to cash out as soon as you depart, you might favor a forced repurchase clause. But make sure you really want a forced repurchase clause before agreeing to one (and note that forced repurchase clauses often say your employer is not required to repurchase your shares).

Beware of the Buried Change in Control Forfeiture Scam

Beware of the buried change in control forfeiture scam!

All options and restricted stock issued pursuant to an IRS qualified plan (most employee equity) are governed by an equity plan (the plan goes by different names) approved by the employer's board of directors and shareholders.

Your employer's equity plan may have a clause buried deep inside it (in the section that describes what happens in a sale or merger) that allows your employer to terminate your option or restricted stock agreement and cancel all your remaining unvested equity if it sells itself or merges into another entity.

You could kill yourself for two years doing a spectacular job, such a fantastic job that you successfully sell your employer for hundreds of millions more than anticipated. If you haven't protected yourself against the buried change in control forfeiture provision and you have an option or restricted stock vesting pro-rata over four years, you might lose two years of unvested equity, when you have done everything you could do for the shareholders of your company.

Who gets the value of your unvested equity when it is forfeited? The current shareholders, and anyone who made sure the provision would not apply to them. The big winners are usually the founders and large equity investors.

Protect against this buried forfeiture clause. Here's how:

- Review very carefully the section in your employer's equity plan that describes what happens to your equity award if your employer is sold or merged into another entity. Usually the section starts out saying that the acquirer may assume your equity award or substitute another substantially similar equity award for yours if it wants to do so. After that, if it says something like, in the event the acquirer does not substitute for or assume your equity award, the equity award may be cancelled (for all unvested shares), then you've got the change in control forfeiture scam. (Note, if your plan provides that all unvested shares accelerate and fully vest if the acquirer does not assume or substitute for the award, then you're golden, there is no scam).

- If you have a buried change in control forfeiture clause, then negotiate with your employer for full accelerated vesting of all unvested shares in the event your unvested equity (e.g., the unvested part of your stock option or restricted stock agreement) will be cancelled in a change in control.
- Another way to negotiate for full accelerated vesting if your option or restricted stock agreement will be canceled in a change in control is to insist your employment agreement contain a clause saying that your equity award can never be cancelled, forfeited or forcibly repurchased without your written consent (unless you stop working for the employer, in which case, you hopefully have accelerated vesting). With this clause, if an acquirer desires to cancel your option or restricted stock agreement on a change in control, it cannot do so, and will probably pay you out on the unvested portion of your award.

Other Protective Clauses and Agreements You Might Want

If you're a CEO or C-Suite Officer, make sure to demand an indemnification agreement from your employer (or if there are indemnification clauses in your employer's corporate governance documents, such as its bylaws or Certificate of Incorporation, make sure your employment agreement incorporates the clauses). A broad indemnification agreement protects you in the event you are sued or investigated for something you do, or are alleged to have done, in the course of your employment.

If you're joining up below the C-Suite level, try to negotiate for an indemnification agreement, but don't be surprised if your efforts are rebuffed.

The law in some, but not all, states requires employers to indemnify their employees. In states that do not provide statutory indemnification for employees, I suggest you and all non-C-Suite officers try harder to secure an indemnification agreement from your employer (or a pro-you indemnification clause in your employment agreement or offer letter).

If you're an officer or director, make sure your employer purchases insurance, and at sufficient levels. Directors' & Officers', "D&O" for short, Employment Practices Liability, "EPL" is the acronym, and Errors & Omissions, commonly known as "E&O," are three important policies. E&O is expensive so your employer may not purchase it. If you're in a specialized field, other types of insurance will be important. For example, if you're joining a medical practice, medical malpractice insurance is probably a must.

If your employer's equity agreements don't already contain one, you may also want a clause that automatically extends the post-termination-of-employment exercise period of your stock option in the event you're prohibited from selling the stock when you exercise your option. Otherwise, you might not be able to exercise the option, or if you are able to do so, will be required to come up with the money to exercise. And you'll take the risk the shares will fall in price after you exercise.

Another really important clause for you to negotiate into your employment agreement is a "no mitigation" clause. This clause says something like, "you have no duty to mitigate any breach by the Company of this employment agreement."

Mitigation is the unwritten legal requirement that obligates you to take certain actions (like find another job) to reduce your damages if your employer breaches your employment agreement. If you fail to include a "no mitigation" clause in your employment agreement, your ex-employer might be able to breach the contract, and thereafter assert that you have a duty in the law to reduce your damages. Your ex-employer might say something like, "I don't really owe you the 'X' I previously agreed to pay you; instead I owe you a much lesser 'Y' because you have a legal obligation to go out and work elsewhere to reduce the contractual losses I'm causing you."

The "no mitigation" clause requires your employer to pay you whatever it has agreed to pay you and provide you the equity and benefits it has agreed to provide you. The "no mitigation clause" gets you X in the example above even if you sit around after your ex-employer breaches the contract.

Will Your Employer Pay Your Attorneys' Fees?

Retaining an experienced lawyer may be the best investment you ever make, particularly if your professional prenuptial agreement saves you when later things go wrong. But hiring a lawyer will undoubtedly cost you money.

If you're an experienced entrepreneur or senior executive, or have leverage in some way, if you ask, your employer may agree to pay for some or all of the attorneys' fees you incur during the negotiation of your employment agreement, separation agreement, or other employment-related contract. If your employer agrees, your lawyer will probably send you a legally or ethically required waiver letter, which, if you sign, allows your lawyer to accept payment of your legal fees from a third party.

I don't believe I've ever met an entrepreneur or executive who declined to sign a third-party payor waiver letter. However, I've met many who decided not to ask for payment of their fees because they decided not to waste negotiating capital on a small ask, when they had much more lucrative requests to make. The decision about what to negotiate for, of course, is yours to make!

Striking Down Your Employer's Attempt to Protect Itself

Whether you think of it as your employer's attempt to protect itself from you, or whether you think of it as pro-employer language, your would-be employer's first draft employment agreement will almost surely feature multiple pro-employer, anti-you, clauses.

Your employer may include a term that says you forfeit all your vested equity if it terminates your employment for Cause. Your employer's offer may feature a provision allowing your employer to cancel your equity award if it sells itself. It may include a clawback clause requiring you to pay your employer back earned and spent compensation under certain circumstances. The definition of Cause may be so broad that you can drive a metaphorical truck through it. The definition of Good Reason may be so narrow that it is meaningless.

The key to defeating all pro-employer, anti-you clauses is first to recognize how harmful the terms may be, and second to strike out the provisions from your employment agreement. It's as easy as that.

The problem, of course, is twofold. If you haven't been mistreated before and don't have friends and colleagues who have been screwed in all the ways possible you might be screwed, then your recognition tentacles may not stand up. The old adage, "once burned, twice shy" only works when you've been burned once.

How do you deal with this? Probably by retaining an experienced lawyer....

The second issue is what to strike and how. If you are going to simply black out the offensive clauses and anything close to them, then you might be able to do so on your own. If not, hire an experienced lawyer to help you.

What Doesn't Matter

My suggestion: first focus on whether your would-be employer is the right place for you. If not, then don't sign up.

Assuming you decide your prospective employer is right for you, my second suggestion: When negotiating your employment agreement, focus on big picture issues that maximize your personal return. They often are: compensation package; equity package; and protection.

Don't get hyped up about all the other stuff, unless, coldly and calculatingly, you decide that some of the other stuff is critical to maximizing your personal return. Unless, of course, you can negotiate the other stuff without losing any political or negotiating capital during the negotiation. That could happen, for example, if your employer doesn't care about some of your less-important asks and gives them to you without a second thought and without attempting to exact a negotiating advantage from its gives.

A good example of a term that sometimes matters a lot, but sometimes matters very little is your "title." Titles really matter in some companies, especially in large mature companies that compensate and provide benefits by levels. The better your title, typically, the better your comp and benefit level.

So, for example, a VP at a 15,000-person employer might be in a "compensation band" that receives more base salary, bigger bonuses, more stock options, and better severance than the senior director receives one or two "compensation bands" below. That same VP may receive less of all of these things than an SVP, one level above. No question, in some companies titles matter.

But in many start-ups, early stage and even mid-stage companies, titles sound nice, but don't really mean much. What really matters is base salary, bonus, equity, and protection. Consider: "does your title really matter?" If the answer is, "no it really doesn't matter," then I say, "Don't waste your time on your title, focus on salary, bonus, equity and protection!"

Things to Remember:

- Concentrate on what matters to you in your employment offer letter or employment agreement, such as position, salary, commissions, bonuses, equity, long-term compensation and perks.
- Watch out for clawback clauses and policies.
- Negotiate your separation package into your offer letter or employment agreement, and consider severance pay and benefits, and accelerated vesting of your equity.
- Beware of the buried change in control forfeiture scam.
- Consider negotiating for your employer to pay your legal fees.
- Strike down pro-employer (anti-you) clauses your prospective employer inserts into your professional prenuptial agreement.
- Don't waste political and negotiating capital on things that don't matter.

10

Now You're in the Game

Top of the World

"I know, I know. Your mother always used to say, 'you can't trust anyone you meet after grad school,'" Butch Haver laughed as he took his best friend Walter Geneva's knight off the Board during their weekly Monday morning chess game.

"You're CEO of one of the largest companies in the world, with thousands of employees at your command, and you don't trust anyone," Butch laughed again. "Funny, but sad."

"I trust my people to do their jobs, you know that," Walter responded. "That's why they are in their jobs. If I didn't trust them, they wouldn't be there."

"But I don't trust them with my personal stuff. You know full well that's what my mother was talking about."

Walter loved the Monday morning chess game more than anything he did at work all week. The game was mellifluous fun. None of the pressures of running a multinational company.

Walter and Butch went back a long way, to the kickball fields of Lorraine Elementary School. Although Walter had friends around the globe that he could call on anytime, he only felt entirely comfortable with his second-grade buddy, a few college and grad school friends, and his wife and college sweetheart, Ellie.

Every chess game, Walter felt he re-learned a simple truth: Butch was closer to goodness, or maybe to God, than he would ever be, for Butch served the community's hungry and homeless as executive director of a small non-profit. This thought, Walter believed, grounded him the rest of the week. As soon as the game ended, Walter was back to reigning as king of the multinational he headed, king as long as the company's Board was happy with him anyway.

"So soon, Hervey?" Butch said to the company's director of communications as he entered the room. "It's not seven forty-five yet, and I'm whipping his ass." Walter and Butch used a chess clock to ensure their Monday morning games always ended by 7:45 a.m.

Walter looked up at Hervey. "What's on my calendar today?"

"You have calls with investors at nine and ten, and with Jake and Chris Greg from 11:00 -1:00 p.m." Jake was the company's CFO, Chris Greg the audit committee chair.

"Next is a one-on-one lunch with Vladimir, 1:00-2:00 p.m." Hervey continued. Vladimir was the company's president and COO.

"Stop. I'm never going to remember any more, plus I need to move things around," Walter said as he punched the chess clock with Butch's offending bishop, the one that had taken Walter's knight, and which Walter had just removed with his pawn. The flag on Walter's clock was perilously close to falling.

"Damn it, I'm going to lose this game on time. This is the third week in a row I'm coming up short," Walter groused.

"Hervey," Walter said. "I want to be with Vladimir from one to five today. I want to discuss my reorg with him and that's going to take a few hours."

"But you have a full calendar, with..." Hervey started to object.

"Then move people around. I've got important things to discuss with Vladimir. The reorg involves a lot of people."

"But," Hervey interjected.

"I don't care, Hervey. Move everything around. And let me lose this game in peace."

"Fine," replied Hervey. He left the room, sat down at his desk, opened Walter's electronic calendar, rescheduled the meeting with Vladimir for four hours, and cancelled the scheduled meetings with the head of the company's European business, previously scheduled for 2:00 p.m., the head of South America, previously scheduled for 3:00 p.m., and the call with the governor's chief of staff, previously scheduled for 4:00 p.m.

The Master of All Those Below

All those directly below you on the org chart are at your mercy, for the most part. You hire and fire. And your superiors will probably back your hiring and firing decisions, your management style and decisions, and just about everything else (that's legal), until the day they relieve you of your responsibilities.

Of course, you need to perform well in your job. That includes managing subordinates. You have a variety of management styles to choose from (e.g., collaborative, micromanaging, hands off). Pick what's right for you, keeping in mind that if the style you choose is not among the most popular ones at your employer, the style you choose should be more successful for you than the most prevalent management styles in use at your employer.

Being a productive manager is not so easy. It requires skills that are very different from others you may have, and probably far different from the ones you need to be a successful sole contributor. Managing a 10-person team is also very different from managing a 50-person team, which is very different from managing a 500-person team.

If you're having difficulty getting the managing down, sometimes an experienced manager/confidante may help. Other times an executive coach might work.

Spend time learning who your subordinates are, especially your direct reports. It will make you a much better manager. And it may help protect you from complaints being lodged against you by subordinates.

I'm not talking about complainers protesting your illegal activities. If you're acting illegally, for example, discriminating, you should be held fully accountable.

What I'm talking about are those criticizing your effectiveness as a manager, capacity to get along with others, ability to collaborate, and other squishy things.

At most companies, your superiors will probably back you until they fire you. But that might not always be the case. Depending on who your boss is, your boss' view of you, the attention given to managerial style and the proclivities of your employer, complaints from subordinates attacking your management style could really hurt you, sometimes even doom you. And watch out for those companies that have a culture of eating their own.

My suggestion: weed out recidivist whiners.

Another suggestion: know your employer and subordinates before deciding how to move forward.

Sdrabat Ale House

"Kumar is a passive-aggressive son of a bitch, but really good at what he does. Depierre is super sleazy. You can't trust a thing he says, but the CEO loves him."

"Mollieman is straight-as-an-arrow, killer at operations, but boring as sh*t to talk to, although there isn't much to talk to him about because he doesn't have anything interesting to say."

"Silvianess is a dynamo, with more business smarts than Kumar, Depierre and Mollieman combined. The CEO is afraid of her because she knows that Silvianess is smarter than she is."

"Valmeg is weird. Johnson, Svalvard, and White are normal."

"To be honest with you, I have no idea what Draculiusclan does all day, but he's another one the CEO loves. It's like hear no evil, see no evil, or whatever that expression is."

"So, what would you do if you were CEO," I asked Sudhir Amir, my ol' college classmate, as I raised a glass of Aristotle Pilsner at our favorite, Sdrabat Ale House. The Monday Night Football game would start in a few minutes.

Sudhir is Kauri, Inc.'s Chief Revenue Officer. Kauri paid him $1.5 million a year in salary and bonuses last year and another $2 million in a mix of stock options and RSUs.

Kumar, Depierre, Mollieman, Silvianess, Svalvard, Draculiusclan, Valmeg, Johnson, and White are the other members of Kauri CEO Hadar Amy's management team.

"What would I do? I would fire Depierre and Draculiusclan and reorg so that Johnson and White report to Svalvard. I would also get rid of Valmeg. I haven't liked the guy since we started together 21 years ago, but he never reported to me so I couldn't fire him. Also, two of the CEO's indirect reports, Zlatavic and Benomio, I would have report directly to me."

Life Among the Equally Powerful

When you and others serve on the C-Suite management team, or when you and others serve as counterparts at some other same level of an organization (e.g., you're all VPs, senior directors, engineers, etc.), then, typically, you can't fire or hire any of the others, and neither can they fire or hire you. If you're on the same level, you don't report to them and they don't report to you.

In the world of the equally powerful, politics (with a small "p") abounds. It's a world where alliances sometimes play, where you may love working with some, may enjoy working with others, may have no feelings about working with ciphers, and where you may detest working with various employees.

The loves and hates play out when one of your counterparts becomes your boss. Then you learn whether your colleague despises you enough to get rid of you.

Over the years, many have consulted me about former counterparts forcing them out of companies they love. Sometimes they should have seen the writing on the wall. But other times the stealth hatred was impossible to discern. Which is all the more reason why a professional prenuptial agreement is a must, especially in large organizations.

Special Projects

A real-world litigator and adjunct law school professor, Secunda Treglia looked out at the students filling her classroom. She was teaching, "The High Technology Ceiling," a course she had created. It was the law school's most popular elective.

"There's much more discrimination out there than you know," Secunda began.

"Plus, you'd be surprised who's doing the discriminating."

"African Americans discriminate against African Americans, but you'll rarely get a jury to understand that. Women regularly discriminate against the 'wrong type' of women, but few juries are going to agree."

"Sometimes the discrimination is in your face, articulated, blatant discrimination, particularly in a world where severance is used to buy off victims."

"Years ago, when I was a new lawyer," Secunda continued, "an exec came to see me. Her name was Summer Sartainer and she had just been made a sole contributor, assigned to special projects for her CEO. Special projects are basically the kiss of death, the way to manage someone off the ship."

"I asked Summer whether she was being discriminated against because of her sex. She was adamant that sex had nothing to do with her situation. She explained, 'They told me that I had reached retirement age, that I could do special projects for a year and after that it was time to leave. They get rid of men the same way,' Summer assured me."

"I was not yet jaded. So, I asked: 'Are you sure they told you that you are too old?'"

"Summer replied emphatically, 'It's company policy to get rid of those over 55.'"

Secunda paused for effect, "They offered Summer a year in special projects, and at the end of the year, a $3 million severance package."

"What could I say?" Secunda asked rhetorically. "I told Summer, 'Your company has bought the right to discriminate against you because of your age.'"

"What did Summer say to me? She said, '$3 million is $3 million.'"

Subordinate to All Those Above

Through my clients' eyes, I've probably seen every type of boss there is, from malevolent screamer, to super nice, to insecure, to paranoid, to ineffectual, to politician extraordinaire, to conflict avoider, to discriminator, to universally loved, and much more.

If you have a good boss, or better yet, a supportive boss, or even better, a supportive boss you love, then that's fantastic. Hopefully you'll flourish (presuming you are good at what you do).

And let me be clear, great bosses exist. I have known multiple instances where engineering teams followed around a beloved leader for an entire career. I have also known many entrepreneurs and executives who are repeatedly begged by former subordinates to hire them at their next opportunity.

The problem, of course, is if you have a bad boss. When you report to a bad someone above, that someone above can make your life miserable, sometimes even end your career at your current employer.

If you have a bad boss, you must get along well enough not to get fired, get yourself assigned to another boss, or find another employer (perhaps you are able to negotiate an exit package as well). However, even at large companies with many possibilities, a bad boss can hurt your ability to transfer to another area. The problem: your bosses' boss will probably back your boss until she fires him. When you've got a bad boss, a professional prenuptial employment agreement can be a godsend.

Bad bosses come in two archetypes: Bad Legal Bosses and Bad Illegal Bosses.

If yours is a Bad Illegal Boss, then your boss should go, or, at the very least, the illegal way you're being treated should cease immediately. There's no place for sexual harassment, or discrimination due to sex, race, gender, age, or religion, to name just a few types of illegal discrimination, nor any other type of illegal conduct. You should not be made a victim. If your boss is a perpetrator, he should be fired.

Age discrimination, sex discrimination, race discrimination, national origin discrimination, and the like happen all the time. Discrimination happens at companies whose marketing says they are the best places to work. Discrimination happens at the biggest companies, at public companies, at private companies, at start-ups, and just about everywhere else.

It's true that many employers have complaint procedures that work the way they're supposed to work. If you work for one of these employers and complain via HR or another approved process, your employer will investigate, and if it finds illegal conduct, your employer will deal with it effectively (including possibly firing the perpetrator).

The employer might even fire the alleged perpetrator without doing a full investigation (because doing so is easier and cheaper than a full-blown investigation or because it eliminates the possibility the perpetrator can do the same thing again).

But that's not the way it always works. It might not even be the way it works most of the time. There are some harsh realities to life in entrepreneurial and corporate America.

One harsh reality: when faced with a complaint, a whole bunch of employers pay a supposed third-party investigator to "investigate." The investigations are often shams that result in the wrongdoer being given a clean bill of health, and you getting screwed (because the sham investigation finds no misconduct). The "investigators" know who pays their bills. The repeat players for the "investigators" are the employers, not you.

Another harsh reality: Filing an internal complaint against your boss is sometimes the "kiss of death." It isn't supposed to be this way, but sometimes it is.

The truth is bosses break the law all the time. And the truth is employers back bosses who break the law all the time.

Another harsh reality: employers sometimes spend fortunes on big name lawyers to defend themselves, outspending you like crazy. And good contingent fee lawyers (you only pay your lawyer if you settle for or win money) aren't going to take your case unless your damages are big.

And, I hate to say it, but the harsh truth is many judges simply don't care.

I've been bringing lawsuits on behalf of wronged employees for over twenty years. But I always raise the possibility of simply moving on when a client has been the victim of illegal conduct. I do so because of these and other harsh realities.

When faced with a Bad Illegal Boss, you must decide whether to complain internally (which is your right!) and possibly externally (filing a lawsuit or arbitration demand), transfer to another job internally (if possible), find another job at another company, take a severance package (if possible) or suffer through the mistreatment.

More often than you might think an executive or entrepreneur (and other employees too) would rather take an exit package and leave his employer than complain or fight, even when the executive has a great case for age discrimination, sex discrimination, or some other type of illegal conduct.

Many high-powered, incredibly successful women – making millions a year! – choose to move on with a separation package, thereby avoiding the stigma of a lawsuit or internal complaint and the time-consuming uncertainty of litigation. They do so even though these incredibly successful women have been told their employer's Board would probably fire the high-profile pig mistreating them.

You can't fault those who decide to accept a lucrative severance package rather than fight the wrongdoing. As a lawyer, how can I advise a successful entrepreneur or executive victimized by age, sex, or some other type of illegal discrimination to file an internal complaint or lawsuit when the employer will pay the entrepreneur or executive lots of money (or other benefits) to leave? Answer: usually, I can't. Putting aside all the other potential downsides, rarely, if ever, can I say with any certainty a court or arbitrator will award more. "A lucrative bird in the hand is worth two possibilities in the bush" to modify the old adage.

Bad Legal Bosses present a different type of challenge. It's not illegal to simply be a bad boss. It's not illegal to mismanage, to display incompetence, to scream (except in certain circumstances).

It's not illegal to be a limpid collaborative manager, nor a condescending micromanager. It's not illegal for your manager to disagree with every smart business suggestion in your repertoire. (Remember that it's not illegal to run a perfectly good company into bankruptcy.)

If you have a Bad Legal Boss, then your options are: tough it out and hope your boss is replaced, you'll be reassigned or promoted; find another person at your company to report to; find another job at another company; and possibly, take a separation package on the way out.

The CEO and the Board

Three rules govern when it comes to CEOs and their boards of directors. There are exceptions, of course, rules are sometimes broken, and certain Boards don't follow the mold, but disclaimers aside, the three rules are:

Rule #1 – The Board will back the CEO until the day the Board fires the CEO.

As a general matter, the Board may listen intently to you, the subordinate, the Board may even believe you, but in most circumstances, the Board will back the CEO (until it fires her). This means if you battle the CEO, especially in skirmishes escalated to the Board, you're likely to find yourself without a job.

Rule #1's general exception is your reporting of the CEO's blatant sex harassment or philandering with subordinates or other embarrassing illegal conduct. When you report these types of wrongdoing, especially in the current climate, Boards often toss CEOs out on their petards (although the public announcement may say the "CEO resigned" for one reason or another).

This is not to say that you'll always lose out if you battle the CEO on issues other than sex harassment or discrimination or other embarrassing illegal conduct. Sometimes you may win, and the Board might even kick the CEO out. But not too often.

Rule #2 – CEOs are very attentive to the predilections of their Board members when the CEO does not control the Board.

One of the Board's jobs is to hire the CEO. Another is to decide on the CEO's compensation. A third is to decide when to fire the CEO. Thus, it's not surprising CEOs are so attentive to their Boards.

CEOs generally know where Board members stand on issues important to the business. Before bringing matters to a formal Board discussion and vote, CEOs often spend time "socializing" Board members with the positions they want to carry the day.

Even moderately sophisticated Boards often receive "Board packages," prepared by management. These may be a set of

PowerPoint slides. Board packages typically contain reports from the various areas of the business. For example, a Board package might include reports from the finance department, product department or business units, engineering department, research and development department, and business operations. CEOs sometimes edit Board packages to present the information, image and proposals they want presented.

Healthy Boards – those working the way they're supposed to – drill down on their companies' businesses, pressing their CEOs for answers when necessary. Doing so is invariably in the best interest of the shareholders. But it's not always in the best interest of the CEOs, especially if job security is a concern. Which is why CEOs use Board packages, socialization and other techniques to keep Board members on their side (or at least, at bay).

Rule #3 – CEOs often try to pack their Boards with loyal Board members.

To avoid the "noise" and "hassles" that independent Board members sometimes bring and to avoid the oversight a healthy Board displays, many CEOs do their best to pack their Boards with Board members friendly to them.

Obviously, when a Board member is the CEO's friend, or beholden to the CEO in some way, that Board member is less likely to buck the CEO.

Pliable Boards make for CEO longevity.

Things to Remember:

- You have tremendous discretion to legally manage those below you (but watch out for whiners).
- Politics abounds among colleagues at the same level.
- The Board will probably back the CEO until it fires the CEO (assuming nothing illegal is going on).
- Your bosses' boss will probably back your boss until your bosses' boss fires your boss (assuming no illegal activity).
- CEOs are very attentive to their Board members and often do their best to pack their Boards with CEO-friendly members.

11

Changes in Control

Will They or Won't They Convert?

"You and your co-founder own a little over 59 percent of the common stock, if I remember correctly."

"59.675%."

"What's your co-founder's name?"

"Tiger."

"Are you and Tiger aligned?"

"Yes, one-hundred percent."

"Are you sure?"

"I sleep with him."

"You didn't tell me that. You're not fighting or getting divorced, are you?"

"What does that have to do with the sale of the company?"

"You and Tiger control a majority of the common stock. If you're fighting or getting divorced, he might not vote with you."

"Not to worry. Tiger will vote his shares exactly the way I tell him to."

"If you say so .... You asked me to look at the docs and tell you what rights you have at the negotiating table."

"So?"

"They can't do the deal without you; with one exception I'll get to. So, it's pretty much all about leverage, how hard you want to negotiate, what your bottom line is, what you'll accept, and how much the preferred investors want to sell the company."

"But we only own 18.18% of the company's fully diluted capital, so can't they do the deal without us?"

"Much to the investors' dismay, I'm sure, the company is a California corporation. In California, each class of stock, voting separately, must approve the company's sale. For Delaware corporations, the law is different, which is one reason why venture capitalists, private equity players and other institutional investors almost always insist on Delaware corporations."

"All of this means," I explained, "you can block the sale of the company if you want to, with one exception. It also means no employment agreement cramdown for you and Tiger because when you say the deal isn't moving forward unless we all first agree on employment agreements for the founders, they'll have to listen to you."

"Can we do that? We're also directors of the corporation."

"That's why you hired my law firm to represent you personally. You wear two hats. My firm looks out for your personal hat. Ritz & Ritz looks out for your corporate hat. You have to ask Ritz & Ritz about all of your fiduciary responsibilities as directors and officers."

"There's one exception that I have to tell you about," I went on. "The preferred shareholders could convert enough of their preferred stock to common stock to take over control of the common, and then vote the common stock whichever way they want to."

"So, we don't really control anything?"

"I wouldn't go that far. The preferred is double participating which means at the closing they receive twice their investment back, and then they participate in the distribution of the remaining sales price pro-rata with the common stock. Once they convert, they lose the 2X return on their investment and would just take pro-rata after all the other preferred shares take a double return. You and Tiger can negotiate aggressively, you can even push really hard, but just not without limits."

M&A and Other Changes in Control

Your employer is going through a change in control when your employer's shareholders, and almost assuredly its board of directors and management team, will no longer control your employer or its assets after the closing of whatever transaction is on the table.

Changes in control come in a variety of flavors. Liquidations are a type of change in control because there is nothing left of your employer to control after the liquidation. Similarly, bankruptcies and assignments for the benefit of the creditors are often changes in control, especially those where creditors wind up owning your employer after the bankruptcy or assignment.

If your employer sells or exclusively licenses more than 50% of its assets, then that is also often referred to as a change in control. Technically, your employer may still control everything having to do with the corporation, but if post-licensing or sale your employer controls less than 50% of its assets, you and others may not want to work there anymore. Your employer's business will probably be fundamentally different than before.

Probably the most famous change in control is the M&A transaction. M&A stands for "mergers and acquisitions." If your employer is undergoing an M&A change in control, then your employer is usually selling itself to a larger acquirer. Technically, the transaction may be a merger or reverse merger, but the end result is that another company will control your employer after the deal closes.

You'll know your employer is going to be purchased because during the change in control, it will usually be referred to as the "target." The company doing the acquisition is, not surprisingly, usually referred to as the "acquirer."

Sometimes you may hear about a "merger of equals," but be wary when you do. The reality is rarely that. One entity and management team are probably going to call the shots after the transaction. And your fate may well depend on which of the "equals" you work for.

Negotiating the M&A Transaction

M&A transactions frequently involve multiple players with different interests that are not always aligned. Often fast paced, M&A transactions sometimes require myriad negotiating hours and multiple all-nighters before they are completed.

Typically, your target employer will enter into a letter of intent, called an "LOI," or term sheet to sell itself (or merge with another entity).

After the LOI is signed, your target employer will probably negotiate a definitive merger agreement, acquisition agreement, or similar sounding contract.

Once your target employer and the acquirer sign the definitive merger agreement, they will almost always close the transaction. The closing is when the money changes hands, the M&A transaction becomes effective and your target employer ceases to be in control of its destiny. The closing may take place weeks or months down the road, depending on many factors, including the size of the transaction, the size of the acquirer and target, integration issues, the need for government approval, and so forth.

Whether you have any influence on the M&A transaction also depends on many factors, including the reason the acquirer is buying your employer (e.g., is your employer being bought for its technology, for its products, for its customers, for its engineering team, to kill your employer's business), who you are, what position you hold, whether you own significant stock, how much the acquirer cares about you, assuming it does, as well as other considerations.

You, as the target's CEO, CFO, founders, significant selling shareholders, will probably (but not always) have a say at the M&A negotiating table. Over the years, however, I've known multiple CEOs, CFOs and founders to be cut out of M&A negotiations, particularly when only spoils remain, and various investors do the negotiating. It seems crazy to leave a CFO out of a sale discussion, but it does happen!

All of this is to say that you could very well be a C-Suite executive of a target and not have a seat at the M&A negotiating table. If you live below the C-Suite level, you almost certainly will not be able to negotiate the terms of the transaction.

Of course, if you have a protective change in control agreement – especially a single trigger one, where benefits are triggered by the change in control itself – you might not care whether you have a seat at the M&A table. That's because you are already protected if your employer disappears in a transaction.

If you do have a seat at the M&A negotiating table, you must be ready for anything and everything, negotiation-wise.

Your interests may be aligned with your employer's key shareholders, but they may not be. Your interests may be aligned with your company's other executives, but they may not. Your interests may be aligned with your employer's founders, but they may not be. Getting the idea?

And these alignments, whether they initially exist or not, may fluctuate throughout the negotiations. You must be ready for multi-party negotiations, marathon sessions and to pay the negotiating price to secure for yourself the best deal possible.

The Rocket Ship

Personal Wealth Manager Platinum Palladium sat down in the conference room at Xerxes Protective Systems, Inc., "XPS" for short. Platinum specializes in managing the wealth of high and very high net worth individuals. Two days before, XPS CFO David Prudent called to tell Platinum that XPS had just agreed to be sold for more than a billion dollars to Barcalsabel, a European multinational looking to expand into XPS' market.

Platinum looked up as the conference room door opened.

"Thank you for meeting me on short notice," David said as he entered the room.

Platinum thought, "no problem at all if I can get any reasonable amount of a billion dollars under management." As he extended his hand, Platinum said, "Happy to meet with you anytime."

David sat down. "When we spoke, I said I would tell you a little bit about the liquid wealth being created by XPS' sale as a background to setting up meetings between you and the key management stakeholders. All are interested in discussing how they should manage their new wealth."

"So, let me get right to it. The three founders, Xerxes, Ella and Pradeep own 48% of XPS, plus or minus. Xerxes owns 25%, Ella 15% and Pradeep 8%. CEO John Dealer has 5% and I have 2%. Other employees own 14% and investors 31%."

"After paying off debt, transaction fees and other expenses, XPS' sale should net the stockholders $1.4 billion."

"Is the math straightforward," Platinum asked, "or are there preferences, rights or other restrictions that affect the wealth calculation?"

"No preferences or other restrictions, other than a 10% indemnification holdback on the net for 18 months."

Platinum knew that a 10% indemnification holdback referred to $140,000,000 of the sales price which would be placed in an escrow account for a year-and-a-half to satisfy claims that might be made against XPS in the 18 months after the transaction closed.

Platinum asked, "Any other individual holdbacks, re-vesting of cash or equity, or something similar?"

"It's a clean deal," David responded. "No individual hold-backs, no re-vesting. I'm not really sure why, but the acquirer hasn't pushed it. Barcalsabel might not want XPS' management team to stay post-acquisition, but it hasn't said that. What I know is that I'll have outlived my usefulness when the deal closes and will only be here long enough to help transition my department to BarcaIsabel's finance team in Europe."

"Here's the spreadsheet of expected post-closing holdings," David said as he handed Platinum a printout of an Excel spreadsheet.

Platinum looked down at the spreadsheet:

Name	Percentage of Sale Price	90% Paid at Closing (Pre-Tax)	10% Holdback (Pre-Tax; Paid after 18 months if no claims)	Total Liquidity (Pre-Tax)
Xerxes	25%	$315,000,000	$35,000,000	$350,000,000
Ella	15%	$189,000,000	$21,000,000	$210,000,000
Pradeep	8%	$100,800,000	$11,200,000	$112,000,000
CEO John Dealer	5%	$63,000,000	$7,000,000	$70,000,000
CFO David Prudent	2%	$25,200,000	$2,800,000	$28,000,000
All Other Employees (273)	14%	$176,400,000	$19,600,000	$196,000,000
Investors	31%	$390,600,000	$43,400,000	$434,000,000

Platinum thought, "Not bad. Let's see how much I can get under management."

He looked up at David and said, "When would you like to set up the meetings?"

The Acquirer – Is it a Savior, Enricher, or Terminator?

What the acquirer does for your employer may be what it does for you, but maybe not. Boy, this sounds abstract!

In other words, just because the acquirer is your employer's "white knight" does not mean the acquirer is your "white knight."

For example, if your employer is in distress and "needs to sell itself," the acquirer may save your employer's business and make your employer's shareholders better off by paying them for the business. Whether you, as an employee, survive is another matter. The acquirer might even terminate your employment at the closing of the deal because it doesn't need you anymore. Has this ever happened? Yes!

In the employer-distress-sale situation, you might wind up with very little or nothing unless you have a management carve out agreement in place, a protective change in control agreement, or another form of retention agreement which pays you to stay employed until your employer closes its sale.

On the other hand, if yours is a successful growing company and the acquirer pays top dollar, or very probably a premium, and you own equity in your employer, then the acquiring company may enrich everybody, including you. Depending on the amount of equity you own and the purchase price, you might be enriched to a point where you gain "financial independence," meaning you can retire whenever you want to.

But even though you are enriched via an M&A transaction, you still may not survive the closing (or not survive very long after the closing). Targets' chief financial officers, general counsels, chief operating officers, vice presidents of worldwide sales, and vice presidents of business development frequently outlive their usefulness at, or shortly after, the close of an M&A transaction.

In addition, a good number of acquirers will not want you, or some or all of your entrepreneur and executive colleagues, to work post-M&A deal for any more time than is required to absorb your former employer into the acquirer. Similarly, your future boss might want you out for no reason other than you threaten him (because you're better than he is), or because you are not his "guy." Never underestimate the value of being someone's (the right) "pick" or being from the right "team," company lineage or company culture.

If you can figure out why the acquirer is buying your employer, it might help you figure out whether you have long-term prospects after your employer's sale.

If your employer is being sold for a reason that does not involve you going forward (e.g., your employer is being bought for the data it has compiled), then how long do you think you'll be employed post-acquisition?

But if your employer's business is being sold intact, and your employer will become a division of the acquirer, you and your management team colleagues may be wanted long term. In this case, your leverage should increase vis-à-vis your employment negotiations for the post-M&A world.

There is also a good chance your employer's acquirer will mess up the acquisition, meaning it will mess up your employer's ongoing business. Billions and billions of dollars have been wasted over the years on failed M&A deals, failed integrations, and failed business models.

If the acquirer messes up post-closing, your employment prospects post-sale could be wiped out.

On the other hand, depending on how the chips fall, it might be the best thing that ever happened to you. For example, if you hang on long enough, and the acquisition turns out to be a disaster, the acquirer may soon be looking to dump your former employer's business, perhaps even allowing you and the other management team members to buy the business back at a song.

The moral of the story is that M&A transactions bring with them so many potential rewards and risks, and it is often impossible to predict how things will play out.

My advice: protect yourself early for the possibility of a post-change in control world, then see what happens. Protection post-change in control starts pre-change in control, hopefully with a protective prenuptial employment agreement. Best is to negotiate for benefits payable or deliverable on a change in control. Second best is to negotiate for benefits payable or deliverable if your employment is terminated by your employer without Cause or by you for Good Reason at any time in anticipation of, on, or after a change in control.

Securing this change in control protection doesn't prevent you from scooping up post-M&A spoils should there be any. If you have leverage, you can always deal for them during the M&A negotiations or post-closing.

Recipe for a Dispute

"We sold Hoogtepunt Gideon Systems for $130 million two years ago, plus a $130 million earnout," Klaus Van Glad, Hoogtepunt's former CEO began.

"Let me guess," I interrupted Klaus, even though this was our first call.

"The acquirer didn't put resources into Hoogtepunt's products, maybe the acquirer said it wanted to go in a different direction, and you're not going to earn most, or any, of the earnout?"

"How did you know?"

"Didn't your lawyer during the sale tell you that earnouts are a recipe for disaster, or at least a lawsuit anyway?"

"We were really certain that Q3, that's the acquirer, would invest in Hoogtepunt's products because it just made business sense to do so."

"Hoogtepunt is a prestige brand, really high end, and there is so much money to be made in prestige products. I mean they paid $130 million in cash for Hoogtepunt."

"Q3's business is every-day products. You can buy their products anywhere. They have a really big business, much larger than Hoogtepunt's. But they failed more than once trying to get into the prestige market."

"So, when they acquired our brand, we figured they wanted to grow their new prestige brand. But they basically flatlined revenue for the past two years. They didn't invest in marketing or sales. They focused most of their resources on another company they acquired about three months after they bought us."

"Whenever targets or management teams come to me with an earnout as part of a sale, I usually tell them to do the deal based on the cash changing hands on day one, and to think of the earnout as an unlikely upside. Not always, of course, but earnout disputes happen a lot."

"Whether you have a case or not against Q3 for breach relating to the earnout, and how strong your case may be, will depend on what the words in the transaction documents say, and on the facts of your situation."

"What do you need me to send you so I can get your opinion on whether or not we have a case?"

Beware of Earnouts

If an earnout is part of your employer's sale, don't start counting your earnout money until the earnout is actually achieved. Earnouts regularly go bad, meaning they are often not paid in full, sometimes never paid at all. Failed earnouts frequently result in post-transaction litigation or arbitration.

An earnout is contingent consideration. It is usually additional money (or equity or something else of value) to be paid at some time or times after the closing (e.g., 1, 2, 3, 4, 5 years later) of the deal, if, and only if, the target's business grows or succeeds in one or more ways that are defined at the beginning of the earnout.

For example, your employer might sell itself so that it becomes a subsidiary of an acquirer for $10,000,000 in cash, plus another $90,000,000 if, within two years after your employer's sale, the gross revenues of the subsidiary increase by a multiple of three. The idea is that you and your fellow employees will work hard to grow the new subsidiary's business because you were a stockholder in your employer and will want to collect your portion of the $90,000,000.

A variation of this: the acquirer offers a bonus, retention agreement or other compensation plan to employees with a significant payout if post-change-in-control productivity of the newly acquired business increases in some pre-defined way. So, in the example above, in addition to the earnout, the acquirer might establish a $90,000,000 bonus pool for employees if the subsidiary's gross revenues increase by three times within the first two years after the acquisition.

An acquirer often pushes for language in the transaction documents that allow the acquirer to run its business any way it wants to, meaning that the acquirer can cheat you on the earnout, if it wants to do so, by directing resources elsewhere.

By contrast, the target and its management team usually attempt to include pro-target, pro-employee language in the transaction documents. That language might require the acquirer to spend a certain amount of money/resources on the target's post-change-in-control business.

An earnout is often a litigation (or arbitration) waiting to happen, especially when the earnout metrics are not met. Those doing the suing (usually the target's shareholders or employees) typically complain that the acquirer didn't devote the resources necessary to give them a fair chance at achieving the earnout. The acquirer usually responds that it acted in good faith and did everything the transaction documents required to achieve the earnout. Now you can understand why the acquirer tries to negotiate language that says the acquirer can run its business any way it wants to during the earnout period.

If you're an employee or shareholder of the target, don't be fooled into thinking during acquisition negotiations (or anytime thereafter) that the acquirer is surely going to continue gangbusters with the target's business just because it's good business for the acquirer to do so, or just because the target is a valuable addition to the acquirer. Even if there's no Machiavellian conniving to avoid paying the earnout, acquirers have been known to mismanage, under-invest, focus elsewhere, or neglect the target's business post-acquisition. The reasons for this are as varied as the ways integrations, businesses and managerial decision-making can go wrong!

The go-forward vitality of an earnout is different for every deal. The vitality depends on the earnout's language and triggers, the quality of the target's business, the facts of the deal, the intent of the parties, and other deal-specific considerations.

If you are negotiating for a significant size earnout, look super closely at the earnout. Coldly and calculatingly consider whether the earnout is ever likely to be paid. Ask yourself: Is the safest (and most realistic) approach to assume the earnout will fail, and the only thing I'll get from the deal is the cash (and other consideration) that changes hands on the day the deal closes?

Bare As ....

"Who represents Churchill Industries in the transaction?" I asked. Churchill Industries and Wolf, Inc. had just signed an LOI for an all cash deal.

"Those guys over on Alpine Lane," Financial Advisor Melon LaPorte replied, referring to the powerhouse Jay, Roshola, Garbanzo & Krinkleman law firm.

Melon doesn't look anything like a Melon, but a questionable cousin years ago decided "Meredith" wouldn't do and "Melon," has stuck ever since.

"My clients are the target's CEO, CFO and Group President. I told them they should retain you," Melon continued. "But sometimes you can't teach people what they need to learn for themselves."

"Ain't that the truth?! But if they don't want help, they don't want help."

"I'm only a financial advisor and I know they need help. Any ideas on how to get them to pay attention?"

"Ask them whether they're indemnified forever into the future for everything they did or didn't do while working for Wolf. When they don't know, ask them to ask the guys over on Alpine Lane."

"Tell them no explanations, no excuses, and that the guys over on Alpine Lane should confirm in writing the following: 'you are forever indemnified as broadly as the law allows by Churchill Industries for everything you did and didn't do while you worked at Wolf, Inc.'"

"When the guys over on Alpine Lane refuse to confirm, tell your clients what might happen to their net worth if they get hit with a very low risk but gigantic dollar lawsuit without any company or insurance to back them up."

The Indemnification Scam

If you're involved in an M&A transaction and have any part of a seat at the negotiating table, or you stand to make any significant money in the transaction, hire an experienced lawyer to help you. Typically, M&A documents are long, full of legalese, and super dull – you'll probably need assistance to decipher them.

Your employer's lawyer is not the answer. She's not looking out for you. She's looking out for the best interests of your employer and its shareholders.

In fact, during the deal your employer's lawyer may be selling you down the river in an indemnification and insurance coverage scam (that's what I call it) you know nothing about. The scam is not likely ever to hurt you (so ignorance may be bliss). But if it does, your damages – right out of your own pocket – could be huge. In other words, very low risk of occurring, but huge potential damages if the scam plays out.

Here's how the indemnification scam works: There is probably a section buried in your employer's definitive merger (acquisition) agreement that says how long the acquirer is obligated to pay for you if you get sued for something you did or didn't do at your target employer. Many merger agreements say the acquiror's obligation goes poof after six years.

This means that if you get sued for something you did or didn't do in the course and scope of your employment six years and a day after the close of the merger, there is no employer, no corporation, no insurance, no nothing to back you up in the lawsuit. By back you up, I mean pay your attorneys' fees, pay the settlement, pay whatever damages a jury might award. In technical terms, there is no one to defend you, hold you harmless or indemnify you.

Consequently, you the target's founder; you the target's CEO; you the target's C-Suite executives are bare (usually only the top executives and founders get sued for acts or omissions in the course and scope of their employment). By bare I mean no company and no insurance to pay anything on your behalf six years and a day after the transaction closes.

So, imagine you, the EVP of Worldwide Sales of Just Sold, Inc. are sued personally six years and eight days after the merger because Just Sold, Inc.'s main product blew-up earlier in the week and destroyed Big Customer, Inc's servers and databases, leading to a $50 million loss. Now imagine that Big Customer, Inc.'s CEO is so pissed at what happened, so pissed that, to his way of thinking, you sold him a bill of goods, that he orders Big Customer, Inc.'s lawyers to sue you for your role in the destruction.

If your employer still existed, you would turn the case over to your employer (or its insurance carrier) and hopefully live happily ever after. But if your employer is no longer around, your employer's acquirer is no longer obligated to indemnify you, and there's no insurance, you'll have to write the check to pay lawyers to defend you, and possibly to settle the case or pay the judgment if there is one.

Do you think that most founders and C-Suite executives of target companies know this? Of course they don't!

When founders and C-Suite executives learn about this during an M&A transaction, they almost always insist that the acquirer indemnify them forever, or alternatively, that their employer buy insurance to protect them down the road.

Don't kid yourself about the lawyers for your target employer telling you about this scam. My experience is they often don't. Either they don't know about it, or more likely, they don't want to slow down the deal by inserting another issue into the deal to be negotiated, and remember, their client is not you the entrepreneur or executive, but the target and the target's shareholders.

When I show up at an M&A negotiating table – which often happens late in the negotiations – I am not always a welcome sight, other than to the entrepreneurs and executives receiving my advice. Explaining how the indemnification-scam works to founders and C-Suite executives invariably *slows down* an M&A transaction because the founders and execs usually say, "wait a minute" and demand protection.

Slowing down a deal usually doesn't sit well with any of the others at the table. The acquirer wants to close the deal to acquire. The target wants to do the deal to get acquired. And the target's lawyers want to do the deal because their target client (or its investors/shareholders/Board) wants to, and because typically they get paid at the closing.

By the way, when the indemnification scam comes up, the acquirer's, target's, and acquirer's and target's lawyers' stories are usually the same: six years is long enough for all the statutes of limitations on all relevant potential claims to expire. Makes sense, doesn't it?

Not really. Any trial lawyer (litigator) worth her salt knows how to beat the statutes of limitations, at least long enough to cost you lots of money in attorneys' fees.

In many places, you beat the statutes of limitations, at least for a while, by pleading "equitable estoppel." That's all you have to do!

Equitable estoppel is legalese for the assertion that a defendant should be stopped from winning its case on the grounds that the statutes of limitations expired because it is not just or ethically right to allow a victory in this way. In other words, the plaintiff asserts that her claims can be brought even after six or more years. If a judge or arbitrator agrees, you could be subject to huge liability!

Let's also not forget about legal claims where the statutes of limitations don't begin to run until the date the wrongs that give rise to the claims are discovered. In some states, for example, the statute of limitation for fraud starts to run only after *the date the fraud is discovered.*

Imagine you live in one of these *date of discovery* states. And imagine, going back to the example above, that Big Customer, Inc. tells the court it only discovered your fraud when the product you sold it blew up. If you have no insurance, no employer and no corporation to pay your attorneys' fees, or the million-dollar settlement Big Customer, Inc. demands, you could have a big problem.

By the way, you might win the lawsuit against Big Customer, Inc. because fraud is a hard claim to win. Your lawyer will celebrate with you! And she will charge you big bucks for her service!

My advice if you are a founder or C-Suite executive of an M&A target: Get a lawyer to read the documents for you.

You Can't Teach People What They Need to Learn for Themselves

"What about the 'employment agreement cramdown' you've told me about?" Financial Advisor Melon LaPorte asked.

"Does Churchill Industries want them to stay?"

"Yes, even the CFO. It's a condition to the closing of the deal that the key executives sign employment agreements."

"I take it they haven't gotten their employment agreements yet."

"True."

"When's the deal supposed to be signed?

"Alpine Lane says in about two weeks."

"You can try to get their attention by telling them about the cramdown, but that may not work because they have no experience with cramdowns. Or they'll say something like the deal can't happen without them and they just won't sign until they are ready or something like that."

"You and I know the momentum of the deal and the pressure to sign will be enormous, and they'll probably not get as good terms as they should, but they don't know that and if they know better than you and won't listen to you, what are you going to do? What's the old line you're always using, 'You can't teach people what they need to learn for themselves?'"

"Touché!"

Last Minute Abuse

"Where's my offer letter?" "Where's my employment agreement," you might wonder over and over again as the M&A negotiation your target employer has been working on for months starts to wind down. You want to know whether you'll be employed after the deal closes and what the terms of your employment will be. You keep thinking, "I need time to negotiate a better deal" because you know the purchaser is not going to offer you its best deal on the first go.

If you ask where your offer letter is, you'll often be told "it's coming," or maybe more honestly, "you'll get it shortly before the deal closes." What's often going on is nothing more than a deliberate attempt by the acquirer to use the momentum of the deal to force you to sign your offer letter with minimal or no negotiation, and with fewer concessions than the acquirer would be willing to live with if you had sufficient time to negotiate. The acquirer does this by sending over your offer letter or employment agreement just days or hours before the M&A deal is to be inked. The acquirer is banking on the expectation that you're not going to throw a last-minute monkey wrench into an M&A deal that the parties are ready to sign. I call this last-minute M&A abuse, the "employment agreement cram down."

Depending on the type of deal, your position at the target and other factors, you might be the crammer or a crammee-victim. If you are a senior-most executive at the target or founder with leverage, you may be the crammer, attempting like hell to cram down offer letters on your subordinate executives, even if they are C-Suite executives.

On the other hand, if your target employer is not doing well, or is being purchased for some reason that does not require top management to be retained, even for a short while post-transaction, then the crammers may be the purchaser (or its M&A team) or possibly your employer's shareholders. That would make you and everyone else at your target-employer, crammee-victims.

Once the offer letters or employment agreements are delivered, whoever is doing the cramming (remember this could be you) wages a full court press on the crammee-victims (this could also be you), pressuring them to sign their agreements and not risk a deal that the crammers assert is a fantastic deal for everyone.

My advice: if you're a would-be crammee-victim, coldly and calculatingly figure out the best way to maximize your personal gain in the transaction. Know that the crammers are doing nothing more than attempting to maximize their gains at your expense!

If you're a crammee-victim, what's your best answer to the employment agreement cramdown? Sometimes the most effective answer is, "no."

If you have the guts to say "no" to the pressure being applied to you and take the risk you might be discarded in the transaction, you may wind up better off.

The negotiation of the M&A deal has probably taken weeks or months, if not years, to get to the very end, which is where the cramdown happens. This means that whoever is doing the cramming is not likely to kill the entire deal over your employment agreement, especially in situations where the acquirer (or your target employer's investors, if they are the crammers) stand to gain a lot in the transaction.

If you, the would-be crammee-victim, push back and say, "no, I won't agree to this, instead I'm going to negotiate a better deal," then your risk (if you don't have a professional prenuptial employment agreement!) is that the crammer responds, "go take a hike, we don't need you anyway."

More likely, however, the acquirer will negotiate a better, sometimes a much more lucrative, employment or related (e.g., option, RSU) agreement with you because it does not want to sacrifice its long-negotiated, large-expected-upside for whatever pittance (as compared to the deal price) it must further compensate you in the deal. This can be especially true if you and other executives with leverage join together and jointly refuse to be crammed.

Brookster & the Vulture Capitalist

To: Robin Jan Hackmeister
From: Brookster Alleys
Subject: 280G & Fatso
Date: 11 April @ 11:00

R.J.,

I just got off the phone with the Company's accountants. They told me that I will have a $20 million parachute payment when the Silverkatzberg transaction closes.

They told me that if I don't agree to a 280G Vote that I'm going to pay about 70% combined in taxes, which includes a 20% excise tax (I should have moved to Nevada years ago – no state income tax 😊). That'll leave me with only $6 million after taxes on my $20 million.

They told me if I do the 280G Vote and it passes, the excise tax goes away, and I keep $4,000,000 more (20%) in my pocket for a total of $10 million in my pocket. That's a lot more money!

But they also told me I need to put the entire $20 million at risk so I could wind up with $0 if the 280G Vote fails. Is that true?

Regards,
Brookster

****

To: Brookster Alleys
From: Robin Jan Hackmeister
Subject: Re: 280G & Fatso
Date: 11 April @ 12:16

Brookster,

Yes, you lose everything if the 280G Vote fails. You are required to sign an agreement that says if the 280G Vote fails, you forfeit your entire parachute payment.

Practically, the 280G Vote almost always passes. In all the years I have been practicing, I know of only one 280G Vote that failed.

The way it works is that 75% of the Company's shareholders entitled to vote (you can't vote because you are putting your parachute payment at risk) must approve your parachute payment. If they do, then no 20% excise tax. If 25.01% or more vote "no," then you forfeit the entire $20M.

Please let me know if you have any other questions.

Sincerely,
R.J. Hackmeister

****

To: Robin Jan Hackmeister
From: Brookster Alleys
Subject: Re: 280G & Fatso
Date: 11 April @ 12:26

I've made so much money for Fatso MaGray and his fellow ingrate investors and now I have to trust them to vote to allow me to keep my parachute payment. Fatso tried to fire me last year – I don't trust him as far as I can throw him, which isn't far ☹.

****

To: Brookster Alleys
From: Robin Jan Hackmeister
Subject: Re: 280G & Fatso
Date: 11 April @ 12:59

Brookster,

For what it's worth, I don't think Fatso is going to vote against the 280G Vote (but no guarantees – I'm a lawyer 😉). Fatso has 10 – 12 other portfolio companies and no entrepreneur would take his money in the future if he votes "no."

Sincerely,
R.J.

****

To: Robin Jan Hackmeister
From: Brookster Alleys
Subject: Re: 280G & Fatso
Date: 11 April @ 13:18

Fatso is a slimy vulture capitalist! I don't trust him! Or any of his henchmen!

How do we get around this? Can I offer to pay Fatso some part of the $4M more I get if the 280G Vote passes to make sure he votes, "yes"?

****

To: Brookster Alleys
From: Robin Jan Hackmeister
Subject: Re: 280G & Fatso
Date: 11 April @ 14:02

Brookster,

No way around the 280G rules. The rules are very strict and the vote must be a real one, without side agreements or deals. Sorry.

Sincerely,
R.J.

****

To: Robin Jan Hackmeister
From: Brookster Alleys
Subject: Re: 280G & Fatso
Date: 11 April @ 14:06

Uggghhh! What do I do? ☹

Big Potential Upside with Small Risk of Disaster: The 280G Vote

Here's the deal with the 280G Vote: Many worry, few suffer. Actually, I don't know any who have suffered, but I am sure they're out there.

So, what am I talking about? I'm talking about an investor vote, that doesn't include you, that might save you 20% in taxes if you're an entrepreneur or executive lucky enough to be in the following situation: First, you're an executive or entrepreneur in a private company. Second, your private company is acquired. Third, you stand to gain a significant amount of money as a result of the acquisition. Fourth, the amount you stand to gain is more than three times your average compensation over the past five years (or if less than five years, however long you have been employed at the target). Your average compensation over the past five years includes all of your comp, including equity.

The amount you stand to gain in the sale if you have equity that is vesting is a complicated calculation. You'll need help with it.

Years ago, Congress decreed that if you earn "too much" in a change in control transaction, what Congress calls a "parachute payment," then the IRS will assess an extra 20% excise tax on all "parachute payments" you receive, or the IRS thinks you may receive.

You can't get out of the parachute payments tax if you work for a public company and your public company is acquired. Sorry, Congress doesn't allow that.

But, if you're an employee of a private company and receiving a parachute payment in an M&A deal, there is one way out of the 20% excise tax. Here's the way: 75% of your target company's voting shareholders (not including you or anyone else slated to receive a parachute payment) vote to allow the parachute payment to you (and the others). Hence the "280G Vote."

Here's the kicker: The 280G Vote requires you to sign a contract under which you agree to *forfeit* (to swear away forever) your entire parachute payment if the 280G Vote fails (less than 75% vote in favor).

Let's say, for example, you could make $500,000 in your pocket with a successful 280G Vote, $300,000 in your pocket if you opt not to participate in the 280G Vote and $0 if the 280G Vote fails – which would you choose? (Note what you actually receive after taxes depends on your overall tax rate.) Imagine how you'll feel if you have to decide whether to go forward with a 280G Vote and you don't think those holding 75% of the vote like you.

There's one technical exception to all of this. Because of the way the parachute payment tax works, you might fall into the small category of employees who wind up with more money in your pocket after taxes, if you earn less money – yes, you read that right; by earning less, there's more after taxes in your pocket! If you fall into this exception, you'll probably need to see an accountant or lawyer.

Did You Say "Golden Handcuffs"?

M&A deals are often very lucrative for the target's entrepreneurs and C-Suite executives. Yes, you might very well receive a great "golden handcuffs" deal as the result of an M&A transaction.

Some acquirers will want you, an important entrepreneur or executive of the target, to keep working for years after the transaction. If that's what the acquirer wants, there's a good chance you'll get a rewarding employment agreement, a "golden handcuffs" deal. That's when you should use your leverage, maximize your returns and negotiate a strong go-forward professional prenuptial employment agreement!

Things to Remember:

- M&A transactions are fast paced with many potential upsides and pitfalls – get help if you have any leverage in the negotiations.
- Earnouts are recipes for a lawsuit – The payment is contingent. Don't count your money until you receive it.
- Watch out for the indemnification scam.
- In an M&A negotiation, watch out for last minute employment abuse (the cramdown).
- The 280G Vote can make life interesting and stressful if your employer is private and you're slated to receive parachute payments.
- If you're going to receive parachute payments and your employer is public, the 20% excise tax is not so interesting, just painful.
- If the acquirer wants you after the M&A deal closes, you may have the opportunity to negotiate a super beneficial go-forward professional prenuptial employment agreement.

12

The Law

The Answer is Still No

"It's been two months since we signed the separation agreement. My money's been in the bank for six weeks. Can I trade now?"

"I haven't been following. Has your ex-employer announced the acquisition yet?"

"Not yet."

"Then you know the answer to the question, unless, for some reason, the deal has become non-material since you signed your separation agreement."

"How long do you think I should wait to sell my stock?"

"The answer hasn't changed, you know that. When you are no longer in possession of material non-public information about your former employer, you can trade. Not before then."

"Just checking."

"Do you want me to tell you what could happen if you trade now?

"I could be liable for civil fines, have the big bad SEC get an injunction against me, and maybe visit the pen for a stay."

"Precisely."

"OK."

"Call me in ten days if the company still hasn't made an announcement so I can tell you the same thing again."

You Mean I Can't Do What I Want?

No, you can't always do what you want at your job. You know that, or you definitely should know it. Laws and regulations limit your and your employer's behavior. Of course, those very same laws protect, depending on your perspective, context and where you find yourself.

Laws that keep you and me and your employer in line (and protect us too!) can be federal (Congress passed them or a federal agency authorized by Congress issued them), state laws (your state legislature passed them or an agency of your state put them in place) or local laws (the local government where you live or work passed them). There's a ton of laws out there that may affect you and your employment. I'll discuss just a few examples here.

I'll start out with some federal anti-discrimination laws. Federal laws prohibit your employer from discriminating against any employee because of the worker's race, color, sex, religion, national origin, or age (if the employee is 40 or more years old). Another federal law prohibits disability discrimination. There are federal laws against paying female workers less than their male counterparts doing the same work and prohibiting discrimination against veterans because they served in our armed forces. States also have a ton of anti-discrimination laws.

Other laws and regulations establish the federal minimum wage and overtime rules. Of course, your state, or municipality, may have a higher minimum wage or more lucrative overtime laws that U.S. law requires. For example, the minimum wage in Alaska, Arkansas and Arizona is higher than the federal minimum wage. Some municipalities are even higher still. New York City and San Francisco are examples. Always pay attention to where you work!

If you work for a large enough employer for a year and you or a family member gets sick, the FMLA, that's short for "Family and Medical Leave Act" requires your employer to give you up to 12 weeks of unpaid leave in any 12-month period to care for yourself or the sick family member. Many federal workers now receive paid parental leave under another law.

There are a host of "whistleblower" laws prohibiting your employer from retaliating against you if you do something your employer doesn't like. For example, the Occupational Safety and Health Act, commonly known as OSHA, forbids your employer from firing or discriminating against any employee who files an OSHA complaint because the employee filed the complaint. Under ERISA, your employer can't discriminate against an employee because she brings an ERISA claim.

Some federal laws not only prohibit retaliation, they provide for the U.S. to pay *bounties* to you if you report your employer's wrongdoing to the U.S. government. For example, the SEC may pay you a *bounty* if you tell the SEC about certain types of financial wrongdoing going on at your company.

Make sure you pay attention to the laws that govern you and your employer!

Absorbed?

"It hasn't been ten days yet. Have they made an announcement? Or are you calling me about a new opportunity?"

"They're going to announce the acquisition this Wednesday before the market opens. I'm going to sell my stock first thing Wednesday morning."

"I wouldn't do that if I were you."

"Why not? Once they make the announcement, I'll no longer be in possession of material non-public information."

"Because the SEC says you have to wait until the market absorbs the material non-public information before you can trade."

"What do you mean absorbs the information? As soon as they announce, everyone will know. They'll be a press release. The info will be on the internet. This isn't the stone ages."

"Unfortunately, there's no hard and fast rule about when a disclosure gets absorbed by the market. But if you trade right away, you'll probably be raising a red flag.

"How long do you think I should wait?"

"Like I said, there's no bright line rule, but in my opinion, you should wait three trading days before selling your shares. Some might say wait two full trading days, but I suggest three."

"What happens if I wait only one day, and sell Thursday morning?"

"You risk the SEC claiming that the material non-public information hasn't been fully absorbed by the market. If that happens, the SEC might come after you for trading while in possession of material non-public information."

"Wouldn't I win?"

"Maybe, maybe not. But why risk it?

"Bastards. I'm sure they told me about the acquisition before firing me so that I couldn't dump my stock."

Securities Laws and SEC Regulations

The securities laws are complex. If you work for (or in some cases, very recently worked for) a public employer, you'll have to pay attention to them. If you don't pay attention, you might find yourself in prison, the subject of an SEC investigation, the defendant in a lawsuit, or fired.

Don't worry too much though. Your employer doesn't want you to run afoul of the securities laws. This is because your employer wants you to continue working for it and also because your employer could suffer if you mess up.

Your public employer should have an insider trading policy to help keep you on the right side of some of the securities laws. And it should have lawyers you can consult (or your employer's general counsel can consult after you consult her) to direct you.

You probably won't be able to do the securities-law-understanding thing alone. Just look at some of the laws you might have to know: Securities Act of 1933, Securities Exchange Act of 1934, Trust Indenture Act, Investment Company Act, Investment Advisers Act, and Sarbanes-Oxley Act. And for each of these laws, the SEC and other government agencies have established tons of implementing regulations.

Foreign Corrupt Practices Act

I don't have a section in this book about how you can't bribe government officials here in the States on behalf of your employer. If you don't know you can go to jail for that, well, I'm not sure what to tell you.

You can't bribe officials of foreign countries either. Not to help your employer here in the States even though the foreign officials have never been to the U.S. and will never be put in jail by the U.S. government. Back in '77, that's 1977, Congress passed the Foreign Corrupt Practices Act, FCPA for short, handing out prison sentences and big fines if you bribe foreign government officials for your employer.

By the way, there are also other federal laws that could trip you up if you try bribing foreign officials. Getting the idea?

Companies that do significant business abroad sometimes have policies you must sign that prohibit exactly what the FCPA and other laws prohibit. In other words, besides going to jail and paying a civil fine, you could also get fired.

Your Employer Might Turn on You

In this vein, if you violate the FCPA or the securities laws (or one of many other laws), your employer may report you to the government for prosecution. Yes, this happens. Would I be writing about it if it didn't?

What are My Rights?

"Debbie told me you would be calling," I had just been connected to Joe Pliskberger, EVP Sales at Medussa Chrion.

Medussa Chrion is a leading internet security company. Debbie, a successful exec I've known for years, told me that Pliskberger was having a tough time with Medussa Chrion's CEO, Zedon Lu, and would be calling. Debbie also explained Pliskberger is very talented, that his teams love him, but his bosses not so much.

"The CEO is retaliating against me and I'm calling to see what my rights are," Pliskberger began.

"Zedon, the CEO, and I have been fighting for months about Medussa's direction," Pliskberger explained. "Zedon is wasting tons of money on an end user strategy that is going nowhere. We have too many marketers, too many product engineers, too many bells and whistles on our products, when this should be an enterprise market and business to business play."

"I've done this before and know how to double this company's revenues, and all I get is grief and constantly changing directions. The constant change keeps our sales teams too thin and misdirected and wastes lots of money."

"I want my stock to be worth something, and it's going to be worthless if Zedon keeps doing what he's doing."

"I couldn't take it anymore so at last week's Board meeting, I laid everything out for the Board. I told them honestly what Zedon's business strategy is, what mine is, why I believe Zedon is driving Medussa into the ground. At the end, I told them they should ask some hard questions about what's going on."

"What did the Board do?" I asked.

"Not a damn thing. They didn't ask me even one question."

"Then what happened?" I inquired.

"Zedon has been ignoring me ever since the Board meeting. Yesterday, a little birdy told me that I'll be fired before the end of the week."

"Who's the little birdy?" I asked.

"The VP of HR is a long-time friend. She suggested me for the job," Pliskberger responded.

"The CEO is clearly retaliating against me," he continued. "Never once during the past months has Zedon given any indication that he wanted to fire me. Then boom. I go to the Board, and he wants me out."

"Do you think Mr. Lu did anything illegal?" I inquired.

"No, nothing illegal. Just lots and lots of stupidity. Zedon has no business sense, at least for our products. He's a hardware guy and we sell sophisticated software. It's not the same."

"Is Mr. Lu well intentioned or is something else going on?" I asked. "Like is he trying to drive the company into the ground to buy it back or is anything else nefarious happening?"

"I have to say," Pliskberger began, "Zedon means well. He's not malicious or anything, just plain dumb when it comes to internet security products."

"Did you tell the Board he's dumb?"

"No, of course not. I just laid out his business strategy and explained why it's not going to work, and then showed them how mine will."

"Is there any discrimination going on? Is Mr. Lu firing you because you are white, or over 40, or not an Asian, or anything like that?

"The only discrimination going on is that the stupid are discriminating against the experienced."

"Unfortunately, it's not illegal in your state for your boss to fire you because you two disagree about Medussa's direction," I began.

"It's only illegal retaliation if your employer fires you because you reported something illegal or something you reasonably believed was illegal going on, for example, illegal discrimination, securities fraud, someone cooking the books."

"What you have here," I continued, "is a pure business dispute between you and your boss. You complained to the Board. And your CEO didn't like it, so he's firing you. No doubt the CEO is retaliating against you because you complained about him to the Board. But it's not illegal to do that."

"Stupid decisions are not illegal. And firing you because you called out his stupidity is not illegal retaliation."

"I suggest you start looking for another job. And see if you can negotiate a good separation agreement. I can help you with that."

But Maybe I Can Do What I Want? – The Business Judgment Rule

I regularly receive calls from entrepreneurs and executives ready to sue because they were fired after speaking up about a better way to run their companies. The firings may have been downright stupid. They might even lead the employers to ruin. And, if the shareholders could vote, they might vote against the firings, and instead, for promotions.

Frequently, however, the firings aren't illegal. If the firings aren't illegal, there usually isn't anything to sue about. And with no professional prenuptial agreement, the fired entrepreneurs and executives are left with nothing more than a back-end business negotiation for a separation package with bosses who may be driving their employers into the ground.

It's not illegal to make really dumb decisions that ruin a business. That's what bankruptcy courts are for. And there are no debtors' prisons in the U.S.

It turns out that as long as you're not doing anything illegal and you're not self-dealing, if you're a director or officer, you have tremendous discretion to do what you want running your business. Your disinterested business decisions, no matter how bad, will almost always be protected by magic, I mean, the business judgment rule, or "BJR" for short.

When you run your company as its CEO or C-Suite officer, the BJR *presumes* that you are acting appropriately. This means if you're the CEO, CFO, president or any C-Suite Executive, the BJR will protect almost any business decision you make.

This also means if your boss is crazy or stupid or incompetent, and you disagree with your boss about your employer's business direction, policy or just about anything else that's legal, your boss can legally fire you.

The BJR basically says that your employer's directors and officers can do anything that's legal in terms of running your company's business, except violate the fiduciary duties they owe your company and its shareholders. These fiduciary duties include the duty of care and the duty of loyalty.

The duty of care means that you can't commit corporate "waste." As a practical matter, it's very difficult to commit corporate waste in a way that breaches the fiduciary duty of care. Plain bankruptcy doesn't do it. A liquidation doesn't usually do it.

For example, if you want to prove "waste" in a Delaware corporation, you must prove that "no reasonable business person would have made the decision," as one Delaware court put it. Good luck trying to prove this!

The duty of loyalty means you must put your employer first – no self-dealing. The duty of loyalty doesn't have much to do with asinine decision making (other than a decision to self-deal).

Without your employer's approval, the duty of loyalty prohibits you from taking an opportunity for yourself or your sister, brother, or nephew that rightfully belongs to your employer. For example, without your employer's permission, don't buy land surrounding the plot of land your employer plans to build its new, as yet-unannounced, headquarters on. And don't have your sister invest (without permission) in the secret deal your employer's joint venture partner just told you about to try and entice your employer to do another joint venture.

One good thing about the BJR from your employee negotiating perspective: If you are negotiating your employment agreement, change in control agreement, management carve-out agreement or just about any other contract, the BJR gives your employer, or prospective employer, almost unfettered reign to give you what you want. It may not do so for any number of reasons, including those discussed in earlier chapters. But if it wanted to do so, your employer or prospective employer probably could meet your demands without running afoul of the BJR.

Things to Remember:

- The laws may keep you from doing what you want to do as an entrepreneur or executive. On the other hand, those same laws may protect you.
- If you break the law, your employer may turn on you and report you.
- If you're not breaking the law and not self-dealing, the business judgment rule allows you to do almost anything you want while you run your company.
- The business judgment rule also allows your employer to give in to just about every possible request (that's legal) you make during employment negotiations if your employer chooses to do so.

13

Gone, Goodbye

What Do You Want to Work There For?

"What do you want to work there for, LK?"

Nobody called Lieberbob Kaputnik by his name. To most, he is "Bob." To me, he has always been "LK."

But whatever you call Lieberbob Kaputnik, you are calling one of the greatest electrical engineering geniuses of our time. Bob has two PhDs, three masters, taught engineering at two of our greatest universities, and published myriad papers. About eight years ago, Bob quit teaching and is now on his second company. You wouldn't know if from looking at him, but Bob is also something of a Casanova. He has six kids by two former wives and a sometimes-current lover.

"Cashflow. My expenses are high," LK answered.

"Got that. But you told me you can land another job in a week or two."

"It'll probably take one or two months to find a job I actually want. It's not like I'm living hand to mouth, but I don't want to spend my reserves. I'm too cheap."

"You don't want to work there do you?"

"I told you, I can't stand getting up every morning to go to work since Riser Kiusata took over. The tyrant is destroying the department. He's a third-tier engineer who doesn't know anything and makes everyone's life miserable."

"If you're ready to leave, why don't you consider asking Kiusata for a severance package."

"Why would he give me anything?"

"You'd be surprised how many executives are relieved when a subordinate they don't want working for them asks for a separation agreement. I can't tell you how many times it's happened."

"I would love to get out of there. What should I do to get a package?"

"You go into Kiusata's office, and tell him, 'Riser, I love this company and I am happy working for you to build our company. But it seems to me, you don't want me here anymore. You're the boss and if you don't want me here anymore, then I don't want to fight you. I'll go quietly as long as you give me a professional separation package.'"

"Do I tell him what I want?"

"Not unless he asks. But you should go into the conversation knowing what you want, just in case he asks. But I strongly suspect he won't. He might say that he wants you to keep working there. But probably, he'll say he needs to think about it or say he'll talk to HR about getting you a package."

"What if he fires me?"

"There's always that risk. If Kiusata wants to play hardball, he'll probably say something like, 'I accept your resignation.'"

"That would ratchet up the animosity, and you'll have to fight to get a separation package. But my experience is that most of the time someone in your position will be offered a separation agreement. You only need one for two months until you can land another job, but I bet you can negotiate for more than two months. I could be wrong, and I've been wrong before, but I bet you'll get three to six months' severance, at least, plus three to six months' paid COBRA. You don't care about your equity because you told me you're not going to exercise your options anyway."

"You know what? That's what I'm going to do. I can't stand working there anymore."

It's Time to Leave

Maybe you'll be lucky and retire at the company you're at. You'll walk out the door, a young 65, or maybe as old as the hinges, a happy camper, on your own terms and kiss the place goodbye. Maybe, you'll even have a defined benefit pension plan to pay you benefits the rest of your life. These types of happy, sometimes quite lucrative, I'm-set-for-life exits do happen.

If you're leaving at the end of the day, on your own terms, congratulations!! You're probably not leaving anything on the table that you don't want left, which is a really good thing!

Similarly, if you have a professional prenuptial employment agreement, and you are asked to leave, then you can probably stick out your hand, and say with a smile, "pay me what you owe me, vest me in what you agreed to vest me. See you around."

If it's time to leave, one way or the other, and you have no professional prenuptial agreement, you may need to rely on a back-end separation negotiation if you want anything when you depart.

How does the back-end separation negotiation happen? Well, I'll tell you!

You're Fired!

Your employer may simply fire you.

As I wrote earlier, in an at-will state (which most are), your employer can fire you for any reason or no reason at all, with or without notice, with or without cause, and with or without explanation (however, your employer cannot fire you for an illegal reason, such as because you're too old).

You can be fired in many different ways. You may be called into a room, with HR present – this might be the first time you've seen HR since you were hired – and given your walking papers. You might even be walked to the door immediately thereafter and told never to return.

On the other hand, your employer might tell you it's terminating your employment, and thereafter give you some time to transition, and move on. Or your employer may tell you that you're being fired on some future date (say in two months), but not require you to come to work anymore.

Few doing the deed these days will tell you, "I am firing you today." "Firing" is too harsh a word for many. Rather, you'll probably be told something like, "your employment is being terminated, effective immediately," or alternatively, effective on some future date. Others will try to sugar-coat the message, perhaps talking in terms of your "transition period," or something similar, but the end result is the same – start thinking about maximizing your exit package and what you'll be doing next!

If you call me after you've been fired, even if it's our first conversation, odds are I'll tell you something like: "you're not alone; fantastic people get fired all the time for all sorts of reasons, including diabolically bad reasons; lots of your colleagues have probably been canned; they just don't talk about it; and lots of people who've been fired have become hundred millionaires."

Sometimes your employer will "let you" resign your employment, rather than call your firing a "firing." This may make you feel better. Or you may believe the optics are better.

Beware: if your employer allows you to "resign" and you want to receive unemployment insurance, then the employer should agree in writing not to dispute your application for unemployment insurance. Otherwise, your state's authorities may deny you benefits because you voluntarily quit (resigned) your employment.

Beware too: if you have Good Reason to resign or termination without Cause clauses in your professional prenuptial employment agreement and you resign without Good Reason (unless your employer agrees otherwise), you probably forfeit the separation benefits you negotiated into your employment agreement.

You're Laid Off, *aka Riffed*

Ah, the ol' lay off, aka reduction in force, "RIF" for short. This certainly sounds better than "you're fired" or "your employment is terminated," doesn't it?

However, whether you are fired or you are RIFFED, the result is the same. You have no job. You are unemployed.

A RIF generally implies that your employer terminated multiple employees' employment along with yours. A RIF can be company-wide, or much more localized, for example, in a business unit, group or department.

Thus, an employer may RIF 25% of its workforce across the company, or 25% of those working in its sprinkler business, or 25% of the marketing department. Perhaps, you can take solace that you are not being terminated for doing a bad job.

Depending on where you live and the size of your employer, the federal WARN Act and state employment laws sometimes require that your employer notify you in advance (e.g., give you 60 days' notice) of your last day of employment.

The law may also require the employer to give you a list of the positions and ages of all those who are being terminated during the RIF as well as a list (by positions and ages, not by names) of all those who survive to work another day. This helps you to figure out whether your employer has discriminated against you because of your age. To protect itself, a shrewd employer terminates employees under 40 years of age when terminating older employees.

Often employers will offer you and all others RIFFED at the same time a uniform separation package, *contingent on you signing a release of claims*. So, for example, your employer may lay you off along with 10% of its workforce, give you and everyone else being laid off 60 days' notice, and thereafter pay you all two month's wages in return for a release.

Reorganization of One

The classic f**k-you firing is the reorganization of one. Your boss comes to you and says something like, "we are reorganizing the department, and your position is being eliminated."

You later find out that only one position is eliminated: yours. Sometimes you discover that a younger-than-you employee has been slotted into the role. Sometimes a-more-white than you employee. Or in Silicon Valley, sometimes a more-Indian-than-you or a more-Korean-than-you employee, depending on who the boss or employer is.

If you're the victim of a reorganization of one, you should think about whether the reorg is just a ruse for firing you illegally (e.g., you're really being fired because you're a woman, gay, Chinese, over 60, etc.). Ask yourself: "what's really going on?"

You Don't Want Me Anymore

More times than I can count, after an entrepreneur or executive tells me their story, I ask them: "why do you want to work at a place that doesn't want you?"

And many times, after hearing what's going on, I say to the entrepreneur or executive: "they're telling you that they don't want you anymore."

"But, but, but ...", the entrepreneur might argue. "They need me .... I'm doing a great job ... I don't understand ..." the executive might say.

No if ands or buts, if they don't want you anymore.

It's irrelevant that they need you, if they don't want you anymore.

It's irrelevant that you're doing a good job, if they don't want you anymore.

It's irrelevant that you don't understand, if they don't want you anymore.

Many times, your boss won't fire you. Instead, your boss makes your working life miserable, hoping you'll quit and go somewhere else.

Why does this happen? For all sorts of reasons. In one case, it may be because your boss is passive-aggressive or a conflict-avoider, but wants you out. In another case, it may be because your boss wants you out, but won't have the support of the "organization" (e.g., his boss, the CEO) so instead he makes your life a living hell.

Your boss' signals might be "subtle," or they might be "screamers." Regardless of the signaling, you might catch every signal, or let's face it, none at all.

There are so many ways your boss can tell you he doesn't want you anymore. One classic is disinviting you from important team meetings. Another classic is leaving you off the org chart.

You might miss the signals, but to me or someone like me, the signals will be loud and clear. I regularly say to new clients, "you should have called me six months ago."

Why might you miss your boss' signals? Because this has never happened to you before. Because you have always succeeded and believe that if you try harder, you will succeed. Because you, like many of us, hear what you want to hear and believe what you want to believe. Because you are in denial.

You know how many times an entrepreneur or executive tells me if I just do this, or I just do that, I should be alright? My answer is usually: "If I went to Vegas and bet, I would give long odds that your life expectancy at the job is limited."

Sometimes the entrepreneur or executive tells me they think HR will fix it. My response is usually: "you should be looking for another job."

When I hear the-company-doesn't-want-me-anymore type of employment ending, more often than not, I inquire, "Why don't you consider asking for a separation agreement?"

If you're ready to ask for a separation agreement and the facts of your situation tell me you can probably ask for one successfully, I would probably tell you to schedule a 1:1 with your boss, and to tell your boss you're not resigning and happy to work forever for him (you do this to protect against a boss "accepting your resignation" even though you haven't resigned), but then tell him, that it appears he doesn't want you, and if that's the case, you will go quietly if he offers you a professional severance agreement.

It might be very strange, even difficult for you to ask for a separation package. But there's a good chance if your boss wants you out that he'll breathe a sigh of relief and offer (or ask HR to offer) you a decent separation agreement.

Squeeze Outs and Power Plays

When your boss doesn't want you anymore and signals you to leave, that's certainly a type of squeeze out, and probably a power play.

To me, however, the "true" squeeze out involves depriving you of your equity, or more accurately, equity in which you have not yet vested. Co-founder squeeze outs repeatedly reoccur, and often result in the squeezed-out co-founder losing significant equity.

I think of "power play" firings as those orchestrated by someone who has a big picture, strategic idea about how to run the company, and gets rid of you because you don't fit into the big picture.

You might think of a big picture power play as a power play *writ large*. And the single boss maneuvering as a power play *writ small*.

At the end of the day, what I've been calling, "you-don't-want-me-anymore firings" and what I've explained are "squeeze-outs and power-play firings" may just be semantics, rather than real differences. The end result of both: they don't want you anymore.

You're Done!

"My boss put me on a performance improvement plan about ten days ago, and I'm calling to see what my rights are."

"What do you do?"

"I'm senior director of marketing. I've been doing a really good job. My performance reviews for the past four years have been 5's, that's 'exceeds expectations.' Eight months ago, the Chief Marketing Officer left, and since then, the new CMO has been ignoring me. I've been working 14-hour days, every day, to show him how committed I am."

"When you say the CMO has been ignoring you, what do you mean?"

"About four months ago, at weekly staff meetings, I became invisible. Whenever I said anything, there was dead silence. When someone else said exactly what I did, there was all this discussion. Two months ago, I stopped getting the weekly emails inviting me to staff meetings. The department went out to dinner three weeks ago, and I wasn't invited."

"Did you ask the CMO about why he's ignoring you?"

"Yes. Twice I told him I can't do my job if he excludes me from meetings and doesn't provide timely feedback. He told me to stop worrying and keep working hard."

"Have you been looking for a new job?"

"It's so hard when you're working 14-hour days. I've got my resume updated finally."

"How long is the PIP?"

"The PIP says I have 60 days to correct my performance and meet the goals."

"How many goals are there and can you meet them?"

"If I can keep up my 14-hour a day pace, I should be able to satisfy eighteen of the goals. But the last two are really subjective. Goal nineteen says I have to support my colleagues with positive and creative suggestions. Goal twenty says I have to perform consistently to management's satisfaction."

"How did they give you the PIP and what did they say when they gave it to you?"

"About 10 days ago, the CMO scheduled a meeting with me. HR was in the room. They gave me the PIP and explained how it works. They asked me to sign it, which I did. They also told me that if I didn't want to go on a PIP, they would give me a separation agreement with five months of separation pay, but if I go on the PIP and fail, then I'll be terminated without any separation pay."

"Did they say anything else?"

"No. What do you think?"

"I think your employment is going to be terminated on day 60 because there's no way you're going to meet the PIP."

"But I've been working so hard. Maybe if I go to 16-hour days, I can do it. 16-hour days are really tough, but for two months I can do anything."

"I don't think you understand. Your employer doesn't want you to work for it anymore. Your boss wants you out of the company forever."

"The reason you're on a PIP is so the company can protect itself if you come back and try to sue it. Your employer will say it gave you every chance in the world to succeed, and you failed, and it has no obligation to keep bad employees on the payroll."

"But..."

"But nothing. Your employer doesn't want you anymore. You may not understand why. You may not agree with it. It may not be fair. But the fact is your boss doesn't want you anymore, and you'll be fired at the end of the PIP."

"Are you sure?"

"Am I 100% sure? No. I could be wrong, and I've been wrong before. But if I went to Vegas, I would give long odds, maybe 100-1 odds, that you'll be fired after your PIP expires."

"If you're not 100% sure, that means, there's a chance."

"If that's your response to what I just said, then I strongly suggest you see a shrink because I can't help you."

"What do you mean?"

"I mean you didn't really hear me and latched on to what you wanted to hear. I can't guarantee you'll be fired, but in my opinion, there's an overwhelming chance that you'll be fired at the end of the PIP."

"So, what do you recommend?"

"I recommend that you start looking for a new job right now. Not tomorrow. Not the next day. Now. As in now, as soon as we hang up."

"I also suggest you seriously consider going in and asking for the separation agreement. You should balance the five months of comp or whatever more you can negotiate and your chances of getting a job when you're not employed against your chances of getting a job before the PIP expires."

"There's also the possibility that the company will offer you some severance at the end of the PIP when it fires you, if you want to put up with being on the PIP for another 50 days."

By the way, I know it's really tough now and you're very upset. And I know you're being mistreated by the new boss. But you're going to be fine. Lots of my clients call me after six months to tell me that getting forced out was the best thing that ever happened to them."

The Kiss of Employment Death

The performance improvement plan, or "PIP" for short. It's the kiss of death! At least as far as your time horizon working for your employer!

If you call me about a PIP, I'll invariably tell you to start looking for a new job. That's probably the only way to protect your downside.

On rare occasions, the PIP is legitimate, and your employer genuinely desires to help you improve your skills and continue as an employee. I've known employees to survive PIPs, and even work for the same employer for a considerable time after satisfying their PIPs.

However, the odds are super stacked against you. The overwhelming number of PIPs are nothing more than a sophisticated employer protecting itself against your potential lawsuit. Mature employers, usually employers who have been sued before, often use employer-protective (and employee-debilitating) PIPs.

The way it works is that the PIP gives you 10, 20, 30 or more goals and a set amount of time, say 60 or 90 days to meet those goals. There is no way you can achieve all of the goals, which is *by design.*

You bust your chops for the 60 or 90 days, and at the end of the time period, your employer says something like, "you only met 18 of the 20 goals we set for you. We told you before you signed on for the PIP that your employment would be terminated if you don't meet all of the PIP's goals. Because you failed the PIP, we are terminating your employment."

If you later sue, your ex-employer will undoubtedly argue to the judge, jury or arbitrator that it gave you every chance to succeed, that you failed those chances, and that it has no obligation to employ subpar employees.

If your employer gives you the choice between a PIP and a separation agreement, your employer is essentially saying to you that it doesn't want you anymore and that the PIP is an artifice to protect itself against you.

My advice: Negotiate a better separation agreement, unless for a cold and calculating reason, staying on the PIP helps you maximize your bottom line (e.g., it's easier to find a job while you are employed, even if you're on a PIP).

If your employer doesn't offer you a separation agreement at the same time as the PIP, you should start thinking right away about asking for a separation agreement. It may be the best thing that ever happened to you!

Fired for Cause, Good Reason Disputed

If you're fired for cause because you embezzled, committed another type of serious crime or did something else really bad, you don't deserve anything extra from your employer on exit.

Sometimes, however, when you have an employment agreement with great severance benefits, your employer will nefariously fire you for Cause even though Cause isn't present or dispute the existence of Good Reason even though Good Reason exists.

I discuss reasons why this might happen in the next chapter. The resulting playing field may be very unfair as your employer uses company funds (which it writes off as a business expense) to support its immoral conduct, whereas you're paying out of your own pocket to recover what is yours (or you'll pay part of what you are owed as a contingent attorneys' fee). Unfortunately, if this happens to you, you'll probably need to retain and pay a good lawyer to help you.

Things to Remember:

- If it's time to leave your employer, you may have no choice in the matter.
- If you get fired, you're not alone. Millions of others have been fired, including undoubtedly, many people you know.
- In case you missed it: If you get fired, you're not alone. Millions of others have been fired, including undoubtedly, many people you know.
- One more time, it's super important: If you get fired, you're not alone. Millions of others have been fired, including undoubtedly, many people you know.
- If you're the victim of a reorganization of one, ask yourself: "what's really going on?"
- Getting fired, forced out, squeezed out, RIFFED, or voluntarily leaving with a back-end separation agreement might be the best thing that ever happened to you!
- Just in case you missed it: Getting fired, forced out, squeezed out, RIFFED, or voluntarily leaving with a back-end separation agreement might be the best thing that ever happened to you!
- A PIP is usually the kiss of employment death.
- If your employer nefariously fires you for Cause or disputes the existence of Good Reason, a good lawyer may be your best bet.

14

Negotiating the Separation Agreement

Erin

"HR wants to meet at 4 ☹," Erin texted.

Some clients have the idea that I'm sitting around waiting for their texts, and I'll respond right away. Erin has been my client for twelve years. I hear from her every time she gets into trouble, rarely before or after. The last two weeks, I've been hearing a lot from Erin.

"U'll get a package. $ to keep you quiet. Maybe U can double dip"

"But I m right 😊! They r acting illegally ☹!"

"They will pay U $, equity & U will sign release & confidentiality agree"

"Can't believe they r doing this"

"I told U when U went 2 bat 4 ur LGBT subordinate & complained vs EVP WWS, they would probably fire U"

"U may b right"

"A Friday 4pm meet w HR usually = firing"

"What to do?"

"Tell them they r breaking the law. Assertive, but respectful"

"R they breaking law?"

"Yes! It's illegal to fire U 4 complaining about discrimination against LGBT."

"I'm at-will employee"

"Told U. Co. is free to hire & fire U anytime, but can't b 4 illegal reason. They r firing U for illegal reason"

"For sure they'll want a release and confidentiality agree," I texted again. "And they'll pay you to go. We discussed this. I'm open at 2 pm if U want to discuss ur options again"

"Will call U @ 2"

Free Severance!?!

If you're an at-will employee and you don't have a professional prenuptial employment agreement, then your employer can fire you at any time and doesn't owe you anything more than your accrued wages, and in some states, your accrued vacation pay.

Put another way, you are not entitled to anything when you're fired. No matter how hard you worked. No matter how much success you achieved. No matter how many hours a week, a month, a year, every year, you worked. Of course, this all assumes there was nothing illegal about the termination of your employment. Re-read this paragraph.

Many times, recently fired or soon-to-be fired employees tell me how responsible they are for their ex-employer's growth and how they deserve separation pay to compensate them for all of their hard work.

That's not the way it works. Your current salary and other comp are to pay you for your work. If you think you're underpaid for building your company, then get a raise. Absent a professional prenuptial agreement (or unpaid wages, unpaid commissions or another type of earned but unpaid compensation), your at-will ex-employer does not owe you a single penny for your past hard work, no matter how good a job you did for the company.

Nevertheless, your employer may, and many employers would, offer you a separation agreement even though they aren't required to do so. You may receive money, COBRA premium payments, accelerated equity vesting and more.

If you don't have a protective employment agreement, but are sufficiently senior, then you may be an easy (likely) candidate for a separation agreement. And if you're a candidate for a separation agreement, you may very well be able to negotiate the terms of your separation agreement.

Your goal is to maximize your return on exit, whatever maximization means for you. Maximization may be more than money, for example, paid COBRA benefits or accelerated equity. You may have other concerns. For example, if not burning bridges is a primary concern, you might settle for "less" financially because "less" is more in terms of not burning bridges.

Your employer's goal on your exit is pretty much to secure your release, shut you up, and in many cases, to pay you as little as possible, provide you as few benefits as possible, and accelerate the vesting of none or as little of your equity as possible.

In one sense, it doesn't matter why your employer offers you severance even though it's not required to do so. What matters to you: that your employer *is* offering you severance and *how much* in separation benefits your employer offers.

However, try to figure out why your employer might be offering severance so you can understand whether, and to what extent, you may have leverage in the back-end separation negotiations.

Your employer could have many reasons for offering you separation benefits. These include the desire to secure a release, to make nice if you're a repeat player, because you're an executive, and to foster its corporate culture and reputation.

Erin[2]

"U were right! 😊😊" Erin was back. She had just met with HR.

"Hard to fire EVP WWS when he beats #s 6 qts in a row," I texted.

"But they know they have a problem," I texted again.

"I told HR they r breaking law & they hurt me bigtime cause I turned down gr8 jobs at their biggest competitor and biggest vendor to work there," Erin texted.

"What did HR do?" I texted.

"VP HR gave me package w 6 months," Erin texted back.

"I said not acceptable like U said & nothing < 1.5 yrs pay, healthcare & vesting. I told HR, no release from me 4 anything less"

"Did HR say anything?" I texted.

"This is reasonable package, blah, blah, blah," Erin texted.

"I repeated, not reasonable, they r breaking law, no release w/o >"

"Just like U said 😊😊"

"So?" I texted.

"Blah, blah, talking head, blah, blah. HR finally said she needs 2 speak 2 people. Said company never does > but will check & get back 2 me on Mon"

Severance Offered to Secure Your Release

I can't think of a time in over 20 years of practice that an employer paid severance or accelerated the vesting of equity or paid COBRA premiums during a back-end separation negotiation without demanding, at the very least, in return, a broad-based release of all claims. It may have happened, but I doubt it.

I have known entrepreneurs and executives to receive separation benefits without needing to sign a release when their employer agreed to provide those benefits in an employment agreement or other contract without, at the same time, requesting a general release of claims.

Usually when separation benefits appear in an employment contract, the employer inserts, "providing that all separation benefits are contingent on employee signing a general release of claims acceptable to the employer," or something similar. But not always.

If you have a contractual right to receive benefits on the termination of your employment without a requirement that you sign a release, your employer may offer you more to secure your release.

Employers want you to sign a general release of claims because it's very expensive to fight a lawsuit, even when the employer is absolutely right. In other words, it's often cheaper to pay you something for the release than it is to spend hundreds of thousands, if not millions of dollars, and considerable time, potentially fighting you in court at a later date.

Severance for You the Repeat Player

Some employers will pay you severance because they might see you down the road, and they want the next meeting to be a smooth one. They believe that you'll have more positive feelings about them if they pay severance as compared to sending you packing empty handed.

Similarly, some employers will pay you separation pay because, even with confidentiality clauses in their separation agreements, these employers believe they'll get a bad reputation if they systematically deny departing employees like you a safety net when they go. A bad reputation may make it harder for your ex-employer to recruit and retain employees.

Severance Offered Because You're an Executive

If you're an executive, especially a C-Suite executive, you expect to receive a "severance package" if you're fired. Executives doing the terminations expect to pay severance. It doesn't always happen. But it does much of the time. That's the culture.

Severance Intended to Reflect Your Employer's Culture

Do you work at an employer with a great corporate culture, where the company really takes care of you?

Your employer probably works hard to make you feel that way. It may have a policy of paying terminated employees like you separation pay and benefits so you and everyone else know, "I'll be taken care of, even if they fire me."

Sharif

"Recruiter told me company has severance plan 4 execs and I'll qualify as Sr. VP," I read the text, but didn't understand until I realized the text was from Sharif Anwar, not Erin.

Also a repeat client, Sharif is as addicted to texting as Erin, although he's not an emoji guy. He's been interviewing for VP Engineering jobs.

"What do U think?" Sharif wanted to know.

"Depends on what the plan says. Send me a copy & I'll lyk," I texted back.

I texted again: "probably an ERISA plan. U need to no what it says so you no how to negotiate ur deal."

"Don't have a copy."

"Ask for 1. It's probably on company's intranet. HR will b happy to send to U."

"What is ERISA plan?"

"Too complicated to explain by text. If U want to no, call me. ERISA plan has upsides & downsides. U need to no what it says & ups & downs be4 you negotiate."

"R U free at 4 pm?"

"Yes, I will call U at this #"

Your Employer's Already-in-Place Severance Plan

If your employer is the type that "cares" about its employees and is mature (in the sense that it has been around a while and has many employees), it may have a guaranteed severance plan in place. Undoubtedly it will be an ERISA plan. ERISA is a federal law, Employee Retirement Income Security Act in the long form.

ERISA plans are formulaic. If you qualify under the plan, you will receive whatever plan benefits you qualify for. There may be different levels of qualifications and benefits. For example, departing employees who have been employed more than 10 years may receive more separation benefits than those employed less than 5 years. Similarly, senior executives may receive greater benefits than junior executives. ERISA severance plans almost always require you to sign a general release of claims as a condition to receiving the ERISA-guaranteed benefits.

I don't want to mislead you. Employers use ERISA plans for reasons other than fomenting a beneficent corporate culture. Some do it simply to help protect the company against employees who want to negotiate more separation benefits, because, as a result of ERISA law, the plans can be difficult to challenge in court.

Erin[3]

"Right again 😊😊!" Erin texted. It's not like I didn't have anything else to do but wait for Erin's texts (or Sharif's for that matter).

"What happened?"

"Like U said, told CEO if he didn't want me fine, but I want 15 months all around."

"He said too rich," Erin continued.

"I said I moved off of 18 mnths & I wouldn't move anymore cause they r breaking law"

"I told him, I know u have a problem. U r protecting phobia for ur #s. & I told him re competitor & vendor offers like U told me"

"What did he say?" I texted back.

"Blah, blah, blah ... blah, blah blah ... but he said 15 months!"

"U told me so 😊😊!" Erin concluded.

Negotiating Severance

Your Departing Leverage

Are you really going to accept the first separation offer your ex-employer or soon-to-be-ex-employer offers you?

What do you think I'm going to say if you ask me? I'm going to say: "Come on!" (assuming you are not dealing with an ERISA-based separation agreement).

Does the other side in any negotiation usually offer its bottom line on the first go? Sometimes. But, rarely.

A back-end severance negotiation is the same as any other negotiation, except the widget being negotiated is the value of your labor, your release.

So, the question then is: what, if any, leverage do you have in the negotiation?

Your leverage may be nonexistent, especially if you have been a "yes-man" brownnoser throughout your career (if you said, "yes," every time you were asked for the past eight years, then your employer is going to expect you to say "yes" to whatever separation agreement it offers you – naturally).

But you may have more leverage than you think.

If you work in a corporate culture that "takes care of its employees" or you're a C-suite executive where separation agreements are the norm, then you start a bad situation (not having a protective employment agreement) with some leverage. If you're offered a bad separation package, at the very least, you can look the executive firing you in the eye, and say, "What you offer is not a professional exit package. I expect . . . ."

You may also have business or legal leverage to bring to your back-end separation negotiation.

If you have legal claims, particularly good legal claims, against your employer (e.g., breach of contract, race discrimination, age discrimination claims) then that's a move in the right direction, in terms of negotiating leverage.

But legal claims are not enough. Equally important: what do you plan to do about your legal claims, and even more important, what does your employer think you're going to do about those claims? Negotiations are often driven by perceptions, not reality.

If your employer believes (say you were a "yes" man your whole career), you will never bring a claim, then you will have less leverage than otherwise – you might not have negotiating leverage until you file a lawsuit!

On the other hand, if you have been a "pain in the arse" throughout your career, you might be able to negotiate more than otherwise, because your employer believes you will file a lawsuit unless you're placated.

It's the Tricky Dick theory of contract negotiations. Back in the days when Communist China was our hated and largely unknown enemy (not a trading partner) with a billion-plus citizens, a gigantic army, and nuclear weapons, our president was Richard Milhouse Nixon, "Tricky Dick" to many.

Tricky Dick was a pro-military hawk, paranoid (crazy) enough to go to war against the communist menace. We the people believed it. And the Communist Chinese believed it.

As a consequence, when Nixon went to China for the first time (for an American President) after the Communist revolution, there wasn't anybody anywhere who believed Tricky Dick was doing so out of weakness. Indeed, some believe that, at the time, only Nixon could have gone to China (because our country wouldn't have trusted anyone other than a paranoid, pro-military hawk to do so).

When the Chinese and Tricky Dick talked turkey, Tricky Dick negotiated for more than others might, in large part because the Chinese never knew what he was going to do. Tricky Dick might launch that nuclear weapon at any time.

Similarly, if your employer thinks you might launch your metaphorical nuclear weapon (e.g., a lawsuit), it may be willing to give you more on exit than otherwise.

You might also have business negotiating leverage along the same lines as your potential legal leverage. If your employer believes that, like Tricky Dick, you might very well hurt (or even destroy) its business if you're not treated well on exit, then you'll probably come away from your separation negotiations with more than otherwise.

For example, if you're EVP of World Wide Sales, know everything about your company's product, you live in a right-to-compete state (e.g., California, Oklahoma, North Dakota....), and your employer believes your goal in life will to be to "f**k it" if it doesn't give you a good separation agreement, guess what? You'll probably get a good separation agreement.

So too, if you're a non-yes-man departing CFO, particularly one exiting a public company. If you know where the financial corpses are, your employer is likely to treat you well on exit. Not always because dysfunctionality does exist. But usually.

Note that over-the-top craziness or unpredictability may backfire on you. If your employer thinks paying you severance won't placate you or that you won't abide by the confidentiality and non-disparagement clauses in your separation agreement, your employer may feel it has no choice but to play hard ball with you.

Only in special circumstances should you threaten a lawsuit. Doing so is often counterproductive. Everybody knows you can file a lawsuit, and your employer already has a perception about whether or not you're likely to do so. The unstated spectra of you filing a lawsuit is often enough.

You should negotiate your back-end separation agreement coldly and calculatingly.

But it's hard to have a cold and calculating perspective with all the emotions, concerns and fears that may be swirling around inside you when your employment is ending, unless you consult someone who is not at the epicenter of the negotiation.

If you're entering into a back-end negotiation, my advice: Engage someone to help you think things through. That person might be a trusted advisor, a shrewd no yes-man friend, an experienced executive or former executive, a mentor, or an experienced lawyer.

Those Other Considerations

"You've been the victim of sex discrimination, plain and simple," I said to Jennifer Bella at the start of our call. Jennifer is the SVP of a Fortune 500 company, heavily recruited just over a year-and-a-half-ago to shake up the business. Incredibly talented, Jennifer is well known in her world. She earns $3 - $5 million a year.

"Your facts are great in terms of having a strong case, but, of course, that's a bummer because you've had to live the facts."

"It's been awful," Jennifer replied. "They hired me to do a job, then started shutting me out when I did my job. I have lots of friends who tell me they love women in the C-Suite, until we speak up."

"The media might think your CEO is great, but he's basically a pig. He's definitely said some things that'll hang him if they get out."

"You've got excellent credentials. You're the only woman on a high-profile management team, other than the EVP of HR, who is usually a woman. If you file a sex discrimination complaint against the pig, there's a really good chance the Board is going to fire him. Plus, you'll be doing a favor for all the women who follow you. The CEO is what, somewhere in his mid- to late 50s, so he could be playing piggy for quite a few more years."

"I don't want to fight," Jennifer replied. "I don't want to burn bridges. I don't want to be known as a woman who files complaints. I'm going to get a good job somewhere else pretty quickly, so I'm inclined to take the package."

"Besides the blatant discrimination, what really burns me up," I said, "is that the separation package they're offering you is half, maybe three quarters, what they would be offering a man. Excuse my language, but it's total 'f**k you on exit' discrimination."

"The CEO's a real jerk. But I just want to move on. I'm sorry."

"Sorry? Don't be sorry. It's my job to tell you the pig is mistreating you, you're being discriminated against, and you have a strong legal claim. Once I tell you that, it's your decision about what to do."

"Are you advising me to fight given that they're paying me $1.4 million to leave, even if it's half or three-quarters of what a man would get?"

"Honestly, no. I can't advise you to put $1.4 million on the line to fight, especially since you don't want to stay working at the company. If you file a complaint, you start out having to win $1.4 million plus attorneys' fees just to break even. I can't tell you that you'll get more than that if you file a complaint, whether internal or in court."

"Help me get the best exit package I can. Hopefully, in a few weeks, I'll be calling you to review a new employment agreement."

The Employer's Leverage

Of course, your employer has leverage in your back-end separation negotiation. For example, there's probably some amount of money that you won't risk losing. When the threshold is reached, you'll sign the release, no matter how badly you've been treated.

There's also huge pro-employer leverage in the at-will nature of your employment. Illegal acts aside, your employer can fire you whenever it wants to and doesn't owe you anything.

In other words, if your employer doesn't want to pay you anything, it doesn't have to. And you will have to sue the employer to get anything from it. Standing alone, this is significant leverage. Who in their right mind wants to sue their former employer … the risk, the time, the cost, the difficultly, the chilling effect, the emotional and financial investment, the hassle factor ….?

What about burning bridges? If you're concerned about this, your employer has a leg up.

What about references? If you want employer references, your employer has leverage.

Your employer may have lots more leverage. For example, maybe you did something wrong, or maybe not wrong, but not totally kosher, and you fear your employer may have claims against you.

As another example, your boss or your employer's CEO may be a Tricky Dick, meaning you are on the receiving end of not really knowing how rational your employer will be, and thus, negotiate for less to avoid the unknown paranoid.

My suggestion is the same as before: Engage someone to help you assess your employer's (and your) leverage in the negotiation.

Mateo

"I met with VP 4 Americas today 4 2 hours like U said I should. He still refuses to pay me my $200K in commissions." I was expecting Mateo's text.

Mateo is a senior sales rep at Medicus Fabrica, Inc., a leading medical device company. Mateo had a strong Q3, but, for no legitimate reason that he or I could discern, Medicus refused to pay him his quarterly commission payment. The dispute had been going on for a few weeks. Mateo has been interviewing for jobs elsewhere.

"He said they'll pay $50K now & give me better plan next qtr.," Mateo texted.

"I said no, they need to pay all now"

"He said I knew plan was capped"

"I said plan doesn't say that. I said we can discuss next qtr formula but I need 2 b paid 4 Q3"

"He said no, plan was capped"

"I said no, it wasn't"

"He said, yes it was"

"Went nowhere"

"Finally, like U advised, I said he is forcing me 2 sue & I will"

"He said do what U have 2 do"

"I said OK & that he'll pay my attorneys' fees cause he's not paying me wages"
"Now I have 0 choice"

"Do U want to negotiate anymore?" I texted.

"No. They r cheating me. It's crazy. They owe me the $"

"Definitely sucks," I texted.

"I would walk away for $175K," Mateo texted.
"But he only wants 2 pay $50K & that's a ripoff"

"What do U want me 2 do?" I texted.

"Sue them. I have 0 choice"

When Things Go Bad – The Lawsuit

I'm a big believer in working things out via a separation agreement and moving on. Life is too short. Often future opportunities are just too great.

But I've brought many lawsuits and arbitration demands over the years because things don't always work out.

Indeed, sometimes, the employer deliberately ensures that things don't work out.

As I wrote previously, in a back-end severance negotiation, it's often best to avoid threatening a lawsuit.

Sometimes, unfortunately, either you or your lawyer will need to do so. For example, when you've been the victim of discrimination or some other wrong, it may be necessary to impress upon your employer that you will sue, unless you are compensated for the wrongs visited on you.

In the start-up world, kings and queens abound, unseasoned in legal matters, unseasoned at listening to advisers, sometimes unseasoned at life, those who think, "nobody is ever going to tell me what to do or how to act." Often, they are those who got rich quick, who are the kings and queens of their corporate domains, where all in their business world kowtow to their brilliance. Sometimes they may even believe that god is on their side. As a result, they may behave economically irrationally, and refuse to negotiate a back-end separation agreement with you even when their lawyers and supposed C-Suite advisors are gently (and possibly repeatedly) suggesting to the royalty that they do so. You may have no choice but to sue.

In the corporate world, particularly at the highest levels, there is sometimes a pervasive arrogance that invites lawsuits. It starts with a belief that you can't hurt them or that they're always right, and if you fight them, they'll spend company money to defeat you.

Your employer may also invite a lawsuit in an attempt to renegotiate your professional prenuptial agreement. Why might your employer do this? Sometimes because it is run by a singularly greedy a-hole. But sometimes, it's simply a Machiavellian attempt to renegotiate down your great professional prenuptial package.

Or it may simply be that your employer does not want to pay you X, or vest you Y because in today's dollars, your package is "too rich." This sometimes happens when your employer doesn't remember what it was like when you started working and doesn't believe you are "worth it" now (after you helped build the company!).

Many times over the years successful clients have called with a story about how their employer is attempting to get out of a deal by asserting that Cause exists to terminate their employment or by disputing that the Good Reason clause has been triggered, when it clearly has been. (This is why you must negotiate a narrow definition of Cause and a broad definition of Good Reason, keeping in mind, of course, § 409A.)

In addition, sometimes an ex- or soon to be ex-employer may say bad things about you in public, or in the marketplace where you are looking for a job. If this happens, then you may need your lawyer to threaten a defamation claim to quiet your ex-employer (or whichever of your ex-employer's employees are making the disparaging statements).

The Separation Agreement

Just as with the anatomy of a prenuptial agreement, *Executive Employment Law* is the place to look for all the clauses that might belong in a specific separation agreement. And here again, you should hire an experienced lawyer to advise you because *your situation may call for more or different clauses.*

Of course, many shrewd, and not so shrewd, employees have negotiated great separation agreements all by themselves, without hiring a lawyer or seeking anyone else's advice. There are many incredibly wealthy, repeatedly successful entrepreneurs and executives who've made millions via back-end separation negotiations without ever hiring a lawyer. If that's you, then that's you.

If that's you, then my advice: make sure, coldly and calculatingly, that that's you.

For the rest of us, in the following pages I write about some key clauses you should look out for in your separation agreement.

However you go about doing so, it's absolutely critical that you understand every word, every clause in your separation agreement *before* you sign the document. Otherwise, you might really lose out vis-à-vis compensation, future rights, or otherwise.

Erin[4]

"😊😊 Love U 😊😊"

Always good to have happy clients, I think as I looked at my phone.

"What did he say?" I text back the way Erin likes it, which is immediately.

"3 yrs. to exercise my options!!!!"

"Not 5?" I text.

"Compromise."

"Had to give him something!!!"

"He will sell or do IPO w/i 3"

"R U sure?" I text.

"Yes! But if company tanks, I save my $!"
"& taxes!"

"Congrats!" I text.

"😊😊😊" Erin texts back.

Make sure the amount of money you're receiving to sign the separation agreement and when it will be paid is clear.

Same is true with accelerated equity. Your separation agreement should state clearly how much accelerated vesting you'll receive, and when you'll receive it.

If you don't want to exercise your stock options right away, then try and negotiate an extended post-termination exercise period (e.g., one, two, three years after the termination of your employment). Doing so may be incredibly valuable. You may not have the money to pay for those options now, or even if you do, you may not want to buy them until you see how your ex-employer performs without you. Or you may not want to, or be able to afford to pay the taxes when you exercise (see your tax advisor about this!).

You may be able to negotiate a net exercise of your stock options, where you "pay" the company that number of shares needed to pay the exercise price for the stock options and taxes. Not all employers agree to this, but some do. If you negotiate a net exercise, make sure all parts of the net exercise are spelled out in the separation agreement, so everybody knows what you'll receive.

Don't forget about your ex-employer paying your COBRA premiums. It can do so via a lump sum. Or your ex-employer might pay your premiums directly to the COBRA administrator or as reimbursements to you over time (see your tax advisor in all cases about whether and how the benefits are taxed).

Are you resigning or being terminated or is yours a mutually agreed upon departure? Your employer may offer you – or you may negotiate – the right to choose the characterization.

Does the terminology really matter? If it does, and you want the separation agreement to say you resigned *and* you want unemployment insurance, then insert a clause that says your employer won't contest your right to receive unemployment insurance benefits.

Is your employer paying for outplacement services? If so, but you prefer that the cash value of services be paid to you instead, ask if your employer will pay you in lieu of paying an outplacement service.

If you have reimbursable business expenses that have not yet been paid, then write what you are owed and when it will be paid into the separation agreement. Otherwise when you sign the separation agreement's release, you may waive your right to be reimbursed.

If you would like to keep your company phone or computer or printer or anything else that belongs to your employer, then make sure your separation agreement identifies the property you can keep, and its value. If you're keeping a company computer or mobile phone, ask the company to clean them of all company property – that way, your ex-employer will have a hard time complaining that you took its confidential property or data on your devices when you left.

If you're an entrepreneur or C-Suite executive, some companies will pay some or all of the attorneys' fees you incur on someone like me to review your separation agreement and advise you on your exit. If you've negotiated for your employer to do so, then write this into the separation agreement. The same is true for any other benefits for which you negotiate.

If there is a clause in your separation agreement that describes the agreements that continue in effect after the separation agreement is signed, then make sure every contract you want to survive is listed. Similarly, in the integration section where it says the separation agreement supersedes and nullifies all other agreements, make sure to itemize all agreements you want to survive.

Your employer is going to want a general release of all claims so that you can never sue it (one less person for the company to worry about). You probably want the release to be mutual so that your employer releases you when you release it. However, most employers will resist giving you a mutual release on exit, although they will sometimes make representations like they have "no knowledge of any claims they have against you and no present intention of suing you."

You're almost always going to want a carve out from your release of your employer. In the carve out, you say that certain of your claims will not be released. For example, the following rights should never (or almost never) be waived, which means you may need to insert a clause into your separation agreement saying you are not releasing them: Your right to indemnification, your right to insurance coverage, your rights arising out of the separation agreement, your rights to exercise, receive, hold and sell your company equity.

I always tell clients they should also insert a clause into the carve out providing that they're not releasing their rights in and to any retirement plans. ERISA says you can't release your right to a 401(k) account via an employer's separation agreement, but better super safe than sorry.

Erin[5]

"What did she say?" I hadn't been off the phone with opposing counsel more than five minutes when Erin's text arrived.

"Clause is out," I texted back.

"😊! What happened?" Erin texted.

"I told her no way," I responded.

"Told her U would not agree to forfeiture under any circumstances"

"Told her it is deal breaker for U"

"Told her company can sue U if U breach"

"& if company proves damages, company will collect"

"Did she fight?" Erin asked.

"She said it's not fair to pay U if U break agree"

"Told her again no way & deal breaker"

"She asked is this last issue"

"I said yes. She said we can make change"

"R we done???" Erin texted back.

"Yes. She will send final agreement later. U can sign by EOD," I responded.

"😊😊😊" Erin texted.

No to forfeiture clauses! You should eliminate all you find. Sometimes the first draft of a separation agreement says that you must pay everything back or give back the value of your equity if you breach the separation agreement. Eliminate the abusive clause – if you breach the separation agreement, then your ex-employer should be required to sue you and if it wins, it can collect its damages.

Similarly, no to liquidated damages clauses, particularly big ones! A liquidated damages clause says that you have to pay your ex-employer some amount of money, for example $50,000, each time you breach the separation agreement. Your ex-employer usually claims it needs a liquidated damages clause because even though your breach of the separation agreement will be devastating, it won't be able to prove (or easily prove) its damages. Big liquidated damages clauses can be terribly abusive, especially if your ex-employer decides to come after you.

There's a whole body of law out there about when too-high liquidated damage clauses are really penalty provisions, and as penalty provisions, unenforceable. But who wants to litigate this?

Your ex-employer should be required to prove material breach of the separation agreement and the extent of its damages, and if it can do so, it should be able to collect damages. Don't let your ex-employer short-circuit the process by shifting the risk to you! Except in unusual circumstances, liquidated damages have no place in a back-end separation agreement.

If you have a non-compete clause in your separation agreement, and you live in a state that permits them, make sure you understand exactly what the clause says before signing on to it.

If the confidentiality clause is too narrow for you, revise it so you can disclose to more people.

If you have a sexual harassment or sexual discrimination case and your employer wants the facts of sexual harassment or sexual discrimination to be confidential, see your tax advisor. You may not be able to deduct your attorneys' fees (depending on the status of the law and IRS guidance), although this may not matter because you may never have expected to deduct them.

Your ex-employer will probably insert a one-way non-disparagement clause into the first draft of your separation agreement obligating you not to disparage (say negative things about) your ex-employer, its products and/or services and a long list of affiliated persons and entities.

The first thing you should do is make the non-disparagement clause mutual, so, at the very least, your employer and its officers and directors don't disparage you.

The second thing you should do is consider whether the non-disparagement clause will hurt you in your future jobs.

This could happen, for example, if you go to work for a competitor. A non-disparagement clause covers truthful statements that put your ex-employer in a bad light. If you're going to compete against your ex-employer, how are you going to say that your new company's products are better than your ex-employer's products? Doing so would be disparagement. Think about what you want to do in the future and see if you can negotiate language that allows you to do it.

Do you believe potential employers, or anyone else for that matter, are going to call your ex-employer for references? If so, what, if anything, do you want your ex-employer to say and who do you want to say it? Whatever you decide, write everything into the separation agreement. If you want a particular person to field inquiries, then write that into the separation agreement. If you want a letter of recommendation, then attach a signed copy of the letter to the separation agreement.

If you have a cooperation clause in your separation agreement, consider making your ex-employer pay you a consulting fee for the time it takes you to cooperate. Also make sure you have the right to decide at what times (e.g., only after business hours, only on the weekend) you are obligated to cooperate. And make sure you're not obligated to cooperate if doing so will hurt your future employment or consulting work (you don't want to be obligated to cooperate against your next employer).

If there is something else that's important to you when you separate, then insert whatever else is important into your separation agreement. A separation agreement is just like any other contract. If it's in the contract, you'll receive it (or have a right to sue to receive it, if need be). If it's not in the contract, you won't.

Things to Remember:

- Find out whether your employer has a pre-existing (ERISA) severance plan, and if so, learn what it says.
- Many employers offer separation pay (severance) and other perks when employment terminates even if there's no contractual right to anything and no ERISA plan! Yours may too!
- If you don't have a professional prenuptial agreement, then try negotiating for a back-end separation agreement.
- If you're fired, RIFFED, or reorganized or squeezed out, try and negotiate for a back-end separation agreement.
- If your employer doesn't want you anymore, consider trying to negotiate for a back-end separation agreement.
- You may have more leverage than you think in a back-end separation negotiation. Consider your leverage and your employer's leverage before beginning back-end separation negotiations.
- Know all the things you can negotiate for in your back-end separation agreement.
- When things go really bad, you may be forced to sue.

15

Reincarnation – What About Running ...?

Billy Ball

"... and so, it is with great pleasure that I invite Nathan Mathew to the mike," Entrepreneurs & Investors Forum M.C. Claybourne Cramer said as he finished his introduction of the technology headhunter king.

"It so great to be here," Nathan began. "Thank you Claybourne and thank you to the Forum for inviting me to speak again this year."

"Not many of you know that I grew up on Long Island, a diehard Mets fan. I remember listening intently on my ol' Blue Bird school bus' radio to the Amazin' Mets in '69. The fight between Mets shortstop Buddy Harrelson and Cincinnati's Pete Rose in the '73 National League Championship is a Long Island legend."

"The Yankees, 'you got to be kidding me,' any true Mets fan would say."

"But there was no denying the George Steinbrenner & Billy Martin show. George Steinbrenner was the international shipping magnate and owner of the famed New York Yankees. Steinbrenner was shrewd, rich, all New Yorker, and also a convicted felon, as his manager once famously remarked."

"The manager: The irascible Billy Martin."

"Five times from 1975 to 1989, Steinbrenner hired Billy Martin to manage his New York Yankees. And five times over those same years, Steinbrenner fired Billy Martin. Steinbrenner was apparently considering hiring Martin for a sixth stint in the dugout, but Martin died in a car crash Christmas Day '89."

"Only in New York? No."

"Only in baseball? No."

"Come 'on, only with brash New Yorker shipping magnates who crave publicity? No, again."

"I can't tell you how many times the Steinbrenner-Martin-like reincarnations of my youth and early adulthood play out in the business world, although, when they happen in the business world, single reincarnations, not quintuple, are the norm."

"Many, many times, I've placed fired executives at companies where the stakeholders in those companies either played a key role in the firing of that very same executive, or stood by while that executive was dismissed."

"So, I'm here to tell you today...."

Didn't You Just Fire Me?

Not infrequently, I discover that a shrewd, experienced client might soon be going to work for a previous ne'er-do-well. By "previous ne'er-do-well," I mean someone who played a role in that entrepreneur's or executive's prior firing, or at least stood idly by while the deed was done.

Early in my career, I first learned the reincarnation-of-business-relationships lesson. As a newbie, I was amazed to learn that a just-fired client was considering working for another business of a guy who had just fired him. I'm no longer amazed.

One of the most famous of firings and re-hirings: Apple Inc.'s firing and re-hiring via acquisition and squeeze-out subterfuge twelve years later of Steven Jobs. I had nothing at all to do with that one. Apple fired Jobs in 1985. Twelve years later it purchased his company, Next Computing, and shortly thereafter, re-hired him as CEO. Jobs drove his once and new employer to be one of the most valuable companies in the world. When Jobs died, crowds stopped by his Palo Alto house to pay homage.

The urge to detest everything and anything associated with your firing makes sense. You would only be human if you thought: "To hell with all these jerks! I never want to have anything to do with them again."

If you must, write off everyone anywhere near your firing. I can't say you're wrong for moving on from a painful exit.

My advice, however: When you get fired, consider *not* burning all your bridges. You never know who may help you in the future, or who you'll see again someday down the business road. The bastard who is X or Y or Z around firing time, may turn out to be a positive player later in your career.

I'm not saying you shouldn't burn any bridges. Too many jerks who fire you, you will never, ever want to see again.

Discriminators, abusers, incompetents, just plain losers, are all on that list.

But if you get fired, there may be "friends," colleagues, associates, businessmen or businesswomen who played a role in your firing, and probably others who stood by and did nothing.

I'm not saying these others should be your best friends in the future, or even any kind of friend, except perhaps, a very marginal one. If they didn't stand by you once, they won't ever stand by you. I get that.

I'm not even saying you shouldn't hate these people forever. That's your choice.

What I'm saying is: if you're going to hate and avoid them forever, then do so coldly and calculatingly.

What I'm also saying is reconsider writing off forever everyone who had anything to do with your firing.

After the initial detestation period, consider how those who played a role in your firing and those who stood worthlessly by may *someday serve you*, how they may *someday help you* maximize your personal returns, whatever those returns may be.

Even if ex-ne'er-do-wells never help you to get another job, they may be able to assist you in some other way: Politics, fundraising, expedited access to tickets … to name a possible few. So, rather than burning the bridge, you might be better off keeping these individuals in the circle of "people you know."

Downtime Might Not Be Too Long

With an MD from Washington University and a BA from hometown Boise State, Katarina Nguen had practiced medicine for only so long as it took to complete her cardiology residency. Immediately after finishing her residency, Katarina took an industry job. She never looked back.

Almost four years ago, Katarina started as Chief Medical Officer at well-funded biotech start-up Llipgib, Inc., "LI" for short. This was Katarina's first CMO role. She really loved her job.

By any measure, Katarina's LI career was a success. Katarina received glowing performance reviews and annual performance bonuses of at least 150% of target for each of her first three years.

Katarina is a straight shooter. Literally. An expert markswoman with any type of rifle, Katarina is a biathlete known more for hitting the target than for her cross-country skiing.

But also, metaphorically. In both her personal and business life, Katarina is honesty in its pure form.

Katarina's big problem started just into her fourth year at LI: About eight months before, LI's CEO resigned to take care of her health and was replaced by Zloty Pula. Zloty wants "yes men and women" on his executive team. Katarina is anything but that.

Within his first few weeks on the job, Zloty knew that he couldn't trust Katarina. She would never jump when he said so. Zloty knew he must get rid of her.

For almost eight months, Zloty made Katarina's life miserable. It was so bad that Katarina could barely do her job. Zloty was hoping that Katarina would resign, but never a quitter, Katarina labored on.

Eventually, Zloty could wait no longer. He told LI's board of directors that Katarina was incompetent and needed to be fired. Zloty told the Board that he had identified an excellent replacement for Katarina.

The Board discussed the termination of Katarina's employment for about seven minutes. Ever the politician, Zloty had greased the skids in a series of pre-Board meeting calls. The vote to terminated Katarina's employment was 5-0. Zloty fired Katarina the next morning.

After the initial shock of her dismissal passed, Katarina decided to take a couple of months off for R&R before looking for a new job. About a week into her break, Katarina was at the firing range shooting targets at 200 yards. During a break, she checked her phone. She had a text.

"Hi, Katarina," the text began. "Hunter from KTM Ventures here."

Katarina was taken aback. Hunter Smith was one of the VC members of LI's Board. Hunter had never texted her before, and he had obviously voted to fire her.

"Hi," Katarina texted back.

"Sorry to hear what happened. It's a shame things didn't work out."

"Same here."

"Do you have time for lunch in the next few weeks?"

"Why? Got a severance package. Not thinking of suing company."

"Good to know," Hunter texted back.

Before Katarina could respond, although she didn't really feel like responding, and might not have, Hunter texted again, "Was hoping you would look at 2 of my portfolio companies. One is looking for a CMO."

"Not understanding. Board voted 5-0 to fire me."

"Bad fit. I think both of my portfolio companies will be a better fit."

Why Don't You Take a Look at Another of My Portfolio Companies?

A special brand of reincarnation takes place in the venture capital world. It goes something like this:

> You're a C-Suite executive working diligently for your VC-backed private employer.
>
> You're doing a great job.
>
> However, for one reason or another your CEO wants to fire you.
>
> You may understand why your CEO wants to do so, for example, if you and the CEO have different visions. Or, you may not understand why your CEO has it in for you given your strong performance.
>
> The CEO approaches the company's board of directors, which might be controlled by VCs, and insists you

> are hurting the company and your employment must be terminated. You can't win this one, except in the most unusual of circumstances (unless of course, you have the votes to replace enough Board members).
>
> Faced with a CEO who wants to fire you, the Board backs the CEO (don't forget the Board will almost always back the CEO right up until the moment when the Board fires the CEO).
>
> The Board vote to can you is *unanimous.*
>
> The CEO then fires you.
>
> A short time after your firing, you receive a text, or an email, or a call, from one of the VC Board members *who just voted to fire you.*
>
> The VC Board member tells you that he hopes you will take a look at another company in his portfolio because it needs a CFO, or VP of World Wide Sales, or Chief Marketing Officer or some other position and you might be right for the job.

The VC pretty much cares about one thing: Good rates of return (earning money) for his limited partners. Limited partners are the investors in the VC's funds.

VC funds frequently kick off millions of dollars in management fees, even if the funds make no money. VC funds have time horizons for the huge management fees they kick off. For example, a ten-year fund might kick off outsize management fees for six or seven years. Thus, to keep the management-fee-gravy train running, VCs must raise capital from investors for future funds. VCs will have a tough time doing so if their earlier funds are unsuccessful.

Hence VCs are always seeking to increase their LPs' returns. If a VC believes you will increase the possibility of stellar returns to another of his portfolio companies, then the VC will consider you for the job, no matter what happened at the company he just voted to fire you from.

The Interview

"To be honest with you, I'm not even sure why the recruiter sent you my way," Daneen, Gordito's president, began.

"Gordito is a holding company," he continued, "with eight separate product lines." Each business is headed by a General Manager, who reports to Daneen.

"Why in the world do you want to be COO of Gordito's automotive manufacturing business?" Daneen is a no-nonsense executive. "Your resume screams start-up. We have more than six hundred fifty employees and do $1.2 billion a year in revenue."

Not the most auspicious start to an interview, Jim Jeep knew. But he was prepared. "The last eight years scream automotive guy. Both start-ups were in the automotive space. I love automotive."

"But both those companies failed." Daneen had done his research. "I realize only one really failed. But the other was sold at a fire sale, which is the same as failing."

Daneen had also read Jim's resume. "I see you worked at some impressive manufacturing companies, but that was more than eight years ago, and none of them made automotive products."

Jim was ready. "These last eight years, I learned that the start-up world isn't my thing. Big manufacturing is my first love."

"That's why I'm such a great fit for Gordito's automotive business," Jim said confidently. "I certainly haven't forgotten how to run a manufacturing business. To me, it's like riding a bicycle. You never forget."

"But what does our business have to do with paper products, faucets and industrial piping?" Daneen asked.

"Everything!" Jim exclaimed.

"I spent 18 successful years in manufacturing before my digression into start-ups. I spent 10 years on Z&Z's paper products team. During that time, we grew Z&Z's manufacturing business from $80 million a year to $1.4 billion a year."

"For three years after that, I was number two at DKA Manski's faucet manufacturing business, where we doubled income."

"After that, I grew J-Lotito's international pipe manufacturing business from $220 million to $650 million in yearly revenue in just over five years."

"Manufacturing is manufacturing." Jim was emphatic. "True, I'll have to learn the ropes of automotive, but once I do, I'm confident I'll be able to grow Gordito's automotive business."

"How are you going to do that?" Daneen queried.

"Can I show you my slides?"

The Public Company is Perfect for You ... The Private Company is Perfect for You

Not everyone is an entrepreneur. You might not be. Not everyone thrives starting their own company. You may not.

You might be better at running small public companies. Or maybe you're better at running mid-size public companies. Or perhaps, at running Fortune 100 internationals.

The reverse is also true. Numerous big-company executives have tried their hand in the start-up world, and failed. Just because you're a terrific manager at Microsoft, General Motors, or General Electric doesn't mean you'll be any good at running a fifteen-person, or thirty-person, or hundred-person private company.

Similarly, many entrepreneurs, small company employees and start-up-loving workers cannot effectively function in a Russell 2000 company, never mind a S&P 500 or Fortune 50 enterprise. That might be you. You may feel choked by the bureaucracy, the politics, the speed at which things are accomplished. Entrepreneurs who sell their companies to large conglomerates or multinationals frequently cannot wait to exit post-close.

Your strengths are your strengths. Your skillsets are your skillsets. You're good at what you are good at. You enjoy what you enjoy.

Similarly, you're bad at what you are bad at. You don't like what you don't like.

It's true that, over time, your strengths may increase. It's also true that, with more experience, your skillsets should expand as well. It's also possible that over time, you will begin to enjoy a type of employer that you never expected to like.

But at the end of the day, you have what you have, you're good at what you're good at, and you enjoy what you enjoy.

The logic here leads to the following, which may be as painful to learn as it is true: Even though you might not realize it, or alternatively, even though you may not want to accept it, you may be a terrible fit for the position you are in. Said another way, you may be so mediocre, or so bad at your job, that you deserve to be fired.

If this is the situation you find yourself in, then consider how large America is, how many different opportunities exist. People make millions selling coat hangers, selling chemicals, selling food.

Just because you're not any good at the job you're in, doesn't mean you won't be great in some other position. Don't despair.

Instead, consider reincarnating yourself. The large public company might be the right place for you. Or maybe, the small private start-up is your thing.

Things to Remember:

- Consider *not* burning all your bridges when you're fired.
- Some of those who fired you, or stood by and did nothing while you were fired, might be able to assist you down the road.
- Sometimes a Board member who just voted to fire you will help you get another job.
- Not everyone is an entrepreneur.
- Not everyone is an executive.
- Not every executive is an entrepreneur.
- Not every entrepreneur is an executive.
- If you're fired, consider how best to reincarnate yourself professionally.
- If you hate your job, consider reincarnating to another job.

16

To Compete or Not to Compete

Uh Oh

"I just received a letter from my last employer, that's why I'm calling," Sparky Zermatt-Blanc-Vail-Creek Dill began.

"Before I hear what happened," I responded, "I have one question."

"Shoot."

"How did you get your name?"

"Everyone asks me that. My father's favorite ski mountains are Zermatt and Chamonix. My mother was a ski bum for four years at Vail and Beaver Creek. I guess they wanted me to remind them of their favorite places. They actually met on a chairlift at Jackson Hole. Dill is my father's last name, so my mother got to decide on 'Sparky' for the spark when I was conceived. They're still married."

"Have you skied all those places?"

"How could I not?"

"Love Jackson Hole. Never been to Chamonix, but I've been to the others."

"But I digress. Tell me what the letter says and what the situation is, and I'll see if we might be able to help you."

"Thanks. Four months ago, I left my job at Adamel Consulting in Miami. I moved to San Diego and took a consulting job at Coronado Consultants."

"From my years in industry, I know that non-compete agreements are illegal in California so I didn't think I would have a problem. But yesterday, I received a letter from Adamel saying they are going to sue me if I don't stop working for Coronado."

"Did you sign a non-compete agreement with Adamel?"

"I guess so. They enclosed the non-compete agreement with the letter they sent me. I don't even remember signing it."

"But why should that matter? I live in California now. I have a California driver's license and I'm registered to vote here."

"Is it your signature on the non-compete agreement?"

"Yes."

"Does Coronado Consulting compete with Adamel Consulting?"

"They're in the same space if that's what you mean."

"Where does the non-compete agreement prohibit competition?"

"North America."

"Are you hoping to sign up some of your clients from Adamel while at Coronado?"

"Two followed me already. I'm hoping at least four more will."

"Did you live and work in Florida when you signed the non-compete agreement?"

"Yes. I lived in Florida for 14 years."

"Look at the 'jurisdiction and governing law section' if the contract has one."

"There's two sections. One says, 'governing law.' Another says, 'exclusive jurisdiction and venue.'"

"Read them to me, slowly, please."

Sparky read the governing law clause: "This contract is governed by the laws of the State of Florida, without reference to its choice of law principals."

"The other one says, 'the exclusive jurisdiction for all disputes arising out of or relating to this contract shall be the state and federal courts in and for Miami-Dade County, Florida and all parties to this contract submit to the exclusive jurisdiction of these courts.'"

"Did you tell Coronado that you signed a non-compete agreement with Adamel?" I asked.

"No, I didn't even know I had. Why should it matter? I know there's no non-competes in California."

"Because Florida non-compete clauses are terrible," I responded. "Florida courts aggressively enforce them."

"And you agreed to be sued in Florida. You just read me that."

"If you want to sue Adamel first here in California before Adamel sues you in Florida, you might be able to void the non-compete clause."

"But you have another potential problem. You didn't tell Coronado about your non-compete with Adamel."

"How could this be a problem?"

"When Coronado was recruiting you, did Coronado employees ever come to Florida, or did you always fly to California?"

"We met once in Miami at a convention. Coronado gave me the offer there. But it took three months of negotiations and cross-country flights to finally sign an employment contract."

"Did you sign a confidential information and invention assignment agreement or something that sounds like that when you joined Coronado?" I asked.

"Yes," Sparky responded.

"You asked, 'how could this be a problem?' I would have to know much more, but it's possible that Adamel might be able to sue Coronado in Florida for interference with contract, the contract being your non-compete agreement."

"It's also possible that Coronado may fire you."

"I have no idea what's in your confidential information agreement or your employment agreement, but one or the other probably contains a clause where you represent that you're not a party to any agreement that would prevent you from working for Coronado. An enforceable non-compete agreement would prevent you from working for Coronado."

"So, what do I do now?"

"Consider hiring a lawyer."

The Powerful Non-Compete Agreement

In most states, employment based non-compete clauses and agreements are the norm. They can prevent you from working in your chosen field for a year or two (or sometimes longer).

In turn, this can have the practical effect of keeping you working in the job you're in, similar to indentured servitude. If you need to feed your family, or pay your mortgage, or you need money over the time period of the non-compete for other purposes, and you do one job really well, then you're not likely to wait on the sidelines a year or two so you can work for another employer.

Non-compete states differ on how harsh they are when they enforce non-compete restrictions. Some states will pretty much enforce a non-compete agreement against you in almost all circumstances, and in many situations where other states would not.

Employment based non-compete agreements are unfair to you (unless, perhaps, you're paid your full compensation package not to work). You should be free to work where you want to work as long as you do so fairly, that is you don't use your prior employer's confidential or proprietary information or trade secrets to compete against it.

There's nothing American or free market about non-compete agreements. They're simply pro-employer restraints on trade. Many supposedly conservative, free-market politicians are pure hypocrites when they support the sanctity of employment-based non-compete agreements, which they regularly do. Similarly, supposedly pro-employee progressive politicians are equally hypocritical when they support employment-based non-compete clauses, which they too regularly do.

Read on for more about non-compete agreements, including states that refuse to enforce them and states that enforce them with conditions.

Garden Leave: Getting Paid Not to Compete

Certain "garden leave" states will enforce non-compete agreements only if the employer pays the employee not to work. New York, for example, will not enforce a non-compete agreement against an employee fired without cause unless the ex-employer pays the ex-employee.

New York's financial services industry is famous for garden leave contracts, which often apply to all types of terminations of employment. They require the ex-employee not to compete for a set number of months (or other time period), and obligate the investment bank, commercial bank, brokerage house, or other financial services firm to pay the ex-employee garden leave the entire time.

The kicker with garden leave states is that garden leave usually means paying only base salary, not bonuses or commissions. Nor usually does garden leave include acceleration of vesting (or provide continued vesting) of any equity. So, the deal isn't as good as you might think.

If you work in a garden leave state, you have leverage, and if you're going to sign up for garden leave, then you should negotiate to be paid your full compensation and full equity vesting during the garden leave.

If you live in a garden leave state which is also an Employee Choice Doctrine state, then you should do your best to negotiate away the potentially onerous forfeiture provisions that result from the Employee Choice Doctrine.

The Employee Choice Doctrine Lives On

Certain states allow employers to sign contracts with their employees that force you to forfeit or pay back benefits (like money or the value of stock) in the event you compete with your employer. These states reason that you have a choice: Don't compete and keep your benefits. Or compete and forfeit/pay back, your benefits. Hence the somewhat overstated name, the "Employee Choice Doctrine."

Imagine an employment agreement that pays you $100,000/year base salary and $500,000 in a yearly "bonus" or "special compensation," with the proviso that if you compete anytime in the first year after the $500,000 is paid, $500,000 must be repaid, if you compete anytime in the second year after the $500,000 is paid, $400,000 must be repaid, if you compete anytime in the third year after the special payment, $300,000 must be repaid, and so forth. Once paid, the base salary is never recoverable, but some portion of the special bonus must be forfeited if you compete at any time in the first five years after it is paid. To make matters worse, the repayment may be in a lump sum on the gross amount paid, not the after-tax amount of the payment.

You'll need to find out whether your state is an Employee Choice Doctrine state. If it is and it matters to you, then you should work hard to negotiate out of your employment agreement all Employee Choice Doctrine clauses. If you don't, you might find yourself tethered to your current employer by the specter of having to pay money back to your employer should you compete.

There are some limits to the forfeiture: You cannot be asked to forfeit your 401(k) account. U.S. law prohibits forfeiture of vested 401(k) benefits.

You Can't Steal Trade Secrets in Any Case

No matter what state you live in, you cannot compete against your former employer with your former employer's confidential and proprietary information or trade secrets.

If you do, you could go to jail. Misappropriating an ex-employer's trade secrets, might violate both your state and United States criminal laws, depending on what state you live in, what you misappropriated, and how you misappropriated the trade secrets. For example, if you violate the U.S. Computer Fraud and Abuse Act or the U.S. Economic Espionage Act when you exit your employer, you risk a 10-year stay in the federal penitentiary.

In most states, some form of the Uniform Trade Secrets Act, "UTSA" for short, makes the theft of trade secrets illegal. If you violate the UTSA, your ex-employer might be able to obtain an injunction against you, prohibiting you from working for your next employer. Your ex-employer may be able to recover damages from you as well. And you might even be responsible for paying your former employer's attorneys' fees.

It's important to know how your state defines trade secrets. In California, for example, your ex-employer's "customer lists" are "trade secrets." Use them – whether in paper copy, an electronic version, or simply memorized – while competing against your ex-employer, and you will have almost no chance in court when your ex-employer seeks an order preventing you from working for your new employer. Your new employer will probably also fire you for using your ex-employer's property while working for it.

And don't forget about the CIIAA or whatever your employer calls the document. The CIIAA contractually prohibits you from ever using your employer's confidential or proprietary information or trade secrets, except for your employer's benefit. If you breach the CIIAA, your employer can sue you for breach of contract in addition to all the other exposure discussed above.

My advice: When you leave your former employer, give everything (100%) back, leave everything (100%) behind. Search your house, your garage, your computer, your car, your boat, your underground safe – are you getting the idea? – for everything that belongs to your former employer. Return it all.

The Aggressive Counterpunch

VIA EMAIL ONLY

Dear John,

My law firm represents Fuerza, Inc. ("Fuerza") CEO Donald G. Gersh in connection with the letter ("Letter") you FedEx'd him regarding the purported concern of XZCMastadon, Inc. ("Masty") that CEO Gersh is misappropriating Masty's trade secrets.

By this letter, CEO Gersh confirms that he is not in possession of, nor does he have under his control, any of Masty's confidential or proprietary information or trade secrets (collectively, "Trade Secrets").

CEO Gersh left all of his Masty Trade Secrets, as well as his Masty laptop computer at Masty's headquarters on his last day of employment. Furthermore, on his last day of employment, CEO Gersh wiped his cell phone and all other personal electronic devices of all Masty Trade Secrets *after* confirming with Masty's IT Department that Masty keeps copies of all of the data on Masty's servers.

While I have tremendous respect for you and your international law firm, your "shot-across-the-bow" Letter is nothing more than a malicious attempt to prevent CEO

Gersh from competing against Masty, *as he has an absolute right to do under California law.*

You have no evidence that CEO Gersh misappropriated any Masty Trade Secrets because, of course, there is no such evidence.

Mr. Gersh took the CEO position of Fuerza, Masty's main competitor, only after Masty's Board passed him over for the CEO position in favor of a less-qualified, younger employee. CEO Gersh looks forward to leading Fuerza's evisceration of Masty in the marketplace in a completely legal and ethical way.

In your Letter, you allege that CEO Gersh "must" be using Masty's Trade Secrets because he formerly served as Masty's Chief Operating Officer and supposedly memorized the Trade Secrets. Your allegation is nothing more than a bald-faced, malicious attempt at invoking the "Inevitable Disclosure Doctrine" to prohibit CEO Gersh from competing against Masty. The doctrine stands for the proposition that an executive of an ex-employer cannot possibly work for the ex-employer's competitor without "inevitably disclosing" the ex-employer's Trade Secrets.

As you know, California courts have ruled that the Inevitable Disclosure Doctrine is not the law in California; therefore, any complaint Masty brings based on the Inevitable Disclosure Doctrine will constitute malicious prosecution, and will subject Masty's decisionmakers, and you personally, to a lawsuit for malicious prosecution.

Before bringing any malicious lawsuit against CEO Gersh, I urge you to consult with the lawyer at your law firm tasked with considering malicious claims its partners are considering filing.

Fuerza and CEO Gersh look forward to their future purchase of whatever Masty remnants remain after Masty concedes that it is unable to compete against Fuerza in the marketplace. May the best company win!

Thank you for your anticipated cooperation.

Sincerely,
Controletta Mishigas
Mishigas, Steve & Rick,
a professional law firm
1 Ferblunget Way
Shtetl, California

Freedom in California, North Dakota, Oklahoma...

Obliterating the Non-Compete Agreement

If you want to compete against your former employer in California, North Dakota, and Oklahoma, go ahead. *You are free to do so* (except in limited circumstances). These states ban employment-based (as opposed to transaction-based) non-compete agreements in employment (although, in Oklahoma, you may be prohibited from soliciting your ex-employer's former customers). Other states are starting to do the same as laws are changing. Massachusetts, for example, has a law describing when non-competes are and aren't enforceable. So, check to see whether your state eliminates or restricts employment-based non-compete agreements.

In no-non-compete states, your employer's competitor might offer you a better employment package than your current employer. It's the big leagues, with freedom of movement and freedom of contracting.

It's even illegal in California to require a prospective employee to sign a non-compete agreement as a condition of employment. This means if a would-be employer requires you to sign a non-compete agreement, then you can sue the would-be employer.

Standing alone, California has the fifth largest economy in the world. *In the world.* We do just fine in California without non-compete agreements. I suspect the same is true in Oklahoma, North Dakota and the other states that refuse to enforce non-compete clauses and agreements. You might wonder why more states don't follow suit.

The fifth largest economy in the world and the other no-non-compete states aside, make no mistake, many people believe that you can't be pro-business unless you believe in the sanctity of non-compete agreements. They are, these people assert, the foundation of a strong economy. While walking down the hallway a number of years ago with an in-house lawyer from a multinational headquartered in a non-compete friendly state, the in-house attorney said to me: "I don't know how anybody does business in California. I can't lock up any of my California employees."

The moral of the story is work in California, North Dakota, Oklahoma or one of the other states that ban (in whole or in part) non-compete clauses in employment if you believe that someday you might want to work for a competitor.

A corollary moral of the story: if you work in a non-compete friendly state, and have the desire and ability to do so, then move to California, Oklahoma, North Dakota or one of the other no-non-compete states. If you can't do that, and you have leverage, make sure your professional prenuptial agreement excludes a non-compete clause, or in the alternative, pays your full compensation as garden leave.

Finally, to avoid the situation where your ex-employer pays you severance over time or vests your equity over time to keep you from competing (if you compete, you lose the separation pay yet to be paid and vesting yet to be vested), your professional prenuptial agreement should focus on lump sum severance payments and immediate equity acceleration. That way, as soon as the release, which your employment agreement will almost surely require, becomes effective and you're paid and vest, you can start work at the competitor.

Relocating to California with a Non-Compete from Another State

I can't speak for other no-non-compete states because I don't practice in those states, but I can tell you about California. Entrepreneurs and executives move to California all the time with non-compete agreements signed with former employers in their former states. These entrepreneurs and executives buy a house in California, obtain a California driver's license and plates, send their kids to California schools, in short, they become one of many million transplants to the Golden State.

And invariably, some take jobs in California with competitors of their ex-employers, thinking that they may compete because employment-based non-compete agreements are illegal in California.

Not so fast.

Which State Rules?

If California law applies to the newbie Californian's non-compete agreement with her former employer (not likely), the California newbie has no problem. The non-compete agreement will be unenforceable as a matter of law. Period.

If the other state's law applies, for example, Minnesota, Florida, or Texas law, then the non-compete agreement will be enforceable in that state. Minnesota, Florida and Texas courts will all enforce non-compete agreements under their own state's law.

A California court will not, however, enforce an out-of-state employment-based non-compete agreement no matter whose law applies. So, for example, a California court will not enforce a non-compete agreement in an employment agreement governed by Minnesota, Florida or Texas law. Not ever.

This makes for the state vs. state brawl.

The Race to the Courthouse Steps: State vs. State and the U.S. Constitution

The entrepreneur or executive California newbie who sues her ex-employer in a California court should be able to obtain a court order from the California court invalidating the foreign state's (e.g., Minnesota's, Florida's, Texas') non-compete agreement. If she does so, then she can work in California against the competitor from the other state.

However, if the ex-employer goes to court in that ex-employer's home state, the ex-employer should be able to secure a court order prohibiting the California newbie from competing. The official document the ex-employer will receive from the out-of-state court is called, a "judgment."

If the ex-employer takes the judgment that prohibits competition to California and asks a California court to enforce the non-compete judgment, *the California court will do so*! Every time.

Doing so is required by the Full Faith and Credit Clause of the U.S. Constitution. That clause requires every state to honor the judgments of sister states.

Who says so? The U.S. Supreme Court.

California public policy against non-compete agreements is so strong that California courts previously refused to enforce other states' judgments when those judgments required enforcement of non-compete agreements. Once the U.S. Supreme Court spoke, however, California courts began toeing the line.

The Full Faith and Credit Clause is just as powerful in reverse. If you secure a judgment from a California court invalidating the other state's non-compete clause, you can take the California judgment to the other state and the other state (for example, Minnesota, Texas, Florida) will have no choice but to enforce the judgment invalidating the non-compete agreement, even though it is valid under that state's law.

This could result in a "race to the courthouse steps." The ex-employer races to secure an injunction against the ex-employee from a court in its home state before the ex-employee races to obtain a judgment from a California court invalidating the non-compete. She who wins first, wins permanently.

The Fraudulent Combo

The New York financial services industry couldn't take the free market for labor on the left coast. So, the banks and brokerage houses began writing into their non-compete-laden employment agreements with California employees, clauses that required the California employee to submit all employment disputes to binding arbitration in New York State under New York law.

The New Yorkers knew that asking you and me to sign a non-compete agreement is *illegal* under California law. But they didn't care. The California Attorney General did nothing. And, few if any, California would-be employees sued because they were asked to sign a non-compete agreement.

Even though it is illegal in California to require you to sign a non-compete agreement as a condition of employment, once you sign a non-compete agreement with an arbitration clause, the agreement becomes immediately enforceable against you. That's because of the U.S. Supreme Court.

It turns out the Supremes hate you and me using the court system. Essentially, they want federal courts rid of as many cases (and as many of us) as possible.

To make a long story short, the Supremes ruled that arbitration trumps just about everything, and states are not free to protect their citizen employees when arbitration is involved.

The Supremes also required courts to enforce all non-compete arbitration awards. In terms of freedom of labor, the Supremes are as hypocritical as the politicians discussed earlier. They are unabashedly pro-employer, and anti-Californian.

So that's how the financial industry was able to enforce non-compete agreements on California employees living and working in California. The New York arbitrator, applying New York law, is happy to render an arbitration award that imposes a non-compete obligation on California employees. The disease spread and other large employers mimicked the approach.

California eventually defended its citizens and economy. The Legislature passed and the Governor signed a law that made arbitration agreements intended to deny Californians the protections of California law or requiring Californians to arbitrate outside California voidable by the employee in most circumstances. The law is a valiant attempt by California's Legislature to protect the fifth largest economy in the world from Washington myopia.

My guess: if it hasn't already done so by the time you read this sentence, the Supremes will someday say that California's law is "unconstitutional."

Things to Remember:

- Watch out for restrictive non-compete agreements.
- Some employers will pay you not to compete.
- Watch out for Employee Choice Doctrine clauses.
- Long live the no-non-compete states! These states ban employment-based non-compete agreements in whole or in part.

- If you move to a state that refuses to enforce employment-based non-compete agreements and signed a non-compete agreement in a state that enforces them, things could become complicated. You might not be able to compete.

17

Going International

Is That So?

"It's great. They're giving me eight percent of the fully diluted capital of Sagarmatha Ltd. And vesting in just three years!" Nem Cateratas was excited.

A supernova in international finance, Nem's algorithms are legendary. I always wonder with all the people in finance these days, how Nem creates so many new winner algorithms. She earns a fortune.

"What is Sagarmatha Ltd. and what will you be doing for it?" I asked.

"I'll be opening Sagarmatha's first office in the U.S. They're a really big player in finance around the world, except here. I'm going to make sure they have a big footprint here too. It's very exciting. I can't wait to start."

"When you say 8% of the fully diluted capital of Sagarmatha, which Sagarmatha? The U.S. subsidiary? A foreign corporation? Where's the mother ship located?"

"I'll be getting 8% of Sagarmatha itself. It's an Andorran corporation."

"With its principal place of business where, in Andorra la Vella?"

"Exactly. You know where Andorra is?"

"You're talking about the only co-principality on the globe? In the Pyrenees, half run by the Bishop of Urgel, Spain and half run by the President of France? Official language, Catalonian. Dates back to Charlemagne, sometime in the eight hundreds."

"That's it. I'm hoping you'll negotiate a good package for me, like last time."

"Be happy to try, but you're going to need an Andorran attorney, or maybe a Spanish or French attorney to give you advice."

"Why?"

"Because, I have no idea which laws apply. I have no idea what it means to own 8% of an Andorran company. I have no idea about what rights you'll have, what responsibilities you'll have. In fact, I don't even know whether 8% ownership will get you anything of value. Never mind if there are liquidation preferences, voting agreements, special Andorran rules for foreigners owing stock."

"Sagarmatha could be worth billions. I just want my 8% of that."

"I understand what you want, but not how to get you what you want in Andorra. You'll need an Andorran attorney for that, unless Spanish or French attorneys do Andorran law too."

"OK, but I want you to make sure my employment agreement is a good one."

"With local attorneys on board, I'm happy to help."

Foreign Law Might Govern Even if You Never Leave the U.S.A.

If you receive any type of compensation, benefits, equity or anything else from a foreign company as part of your employment, then you may be subject to the laws of the country where the foreign company is located. Yes, you might be subject to foreign laws even if you live and work in Omaha, Nebraska, and never leave the United States.

This might happen if you work directly for a foreign employer. It might also happen if you're employed by the subsidiary of a foreign corporation.

If you don't know how the foreign laws might affect you, you better find out. Otherwise, you might not receive what you think you should be receiving.

For example, if you earn stock in a private Swiss concern or a private Chinese corporation or a private Korean entity, you must ask yourself: what is the value to me of the Swiss or Chinese or Korean stock?

If your answer is "stock is stock" or "it's probably the same as stock in the U.S.," you sound like you're guessing. If you're guessing, you might be right, or you might be wrong.

Without consulting an expert in the private equity of whatever foreign company you'll receive equity in, you can't possibly know the value of the equity. Equity in a foreign company might carry different rights and obligations than in the U.S. Tax, securities, employment and contract laws may affect your foreign equity in ways you never imagined.

If you don't know: protect yourself, get a lawyer.

Even if the stock you'll earn trades on a foreign stock exchange, like the NYSE Euronext, Buenos Aires Stock Exchange or the Tel Aviv Stock Exchange, stop and consider before taking stock as part of your comp. First, find out the difference, if any, between publicly traded stock in the foreign country and stock trading in the U.S.

Similarly, if you'll receive bonuses or commissions or other types of compensation or benefits from a corporation in another country, you should know exactly what you'll be receiving and how whatever you'll be receiving is calculated *before you sign on with your new employer*. That is, if you care about knowing everything you'll be earning when you start work.

Taxes Anyone?

"Long time no talk Aditi! To what do I owe the pleasure of your call?"

"I'm not sure if you remember, but you wrote me a great employment contract five years ago."

"Of course, I remember. How's Psarouthak International been treating you?"

"Things are going great! I've been hitting it out of the park as GM. Now they've asked me to relocate to Europe for three years to run European operations."

"Is that a step up?"

"They say I need a stint abroad, and that'll put me in line for a promotion, maybe to COO or CEO."

"Wow, that's great!"

"The thing is, Psarouthak wants me to relocate to Stockholm where the top tax rate is about 57%, whereas, taxes here are much less."

"What do you make these days?"

"A million a year, not including stock and LTIPs."

"Combined state and federal taxes in Chicagoland are about 42% in the highest tax bracket. So, you'll pay an extra $150,000 in taxes, more or less, depending on how the tax brackets are graduated."

"I've been making at least a million in stock every year since joining, and that's probably at least another $150,000 in extra taxes."

"Doesn't Psarouthak pay you more for working abroad or have some type of expat tax equalization package?"

"Psarouthak has a relocation package that talks about making me whole for the additional taxes I'll owe, but I don't understand everything. That's why I'm calling. Can you review the relo package for me?"

"I would love to work with you again Aditi! I can review most of the relo package and explain it to you. But, for tax advice, I'll send you the names of three tax lawyers and three top notch CPAs and the links to their bios. Pick one, and we'll arrange a call for you. Or you can call them directly if you want."

Things to Consider When You Work Outside the States

Will you be paid in euros, pounds, pesetas, kroner or some other currency? If so, make sure you consider how fluctuations in exchange rates may affect you.

For example, if you're paying off a mortgage here in the U.S. and the exchange rate moves against you, your mortgage payment may appear a lot more expensive than it did before you took the job. On the other hand, if you eat, breathe, sleep and save in a foreign currency, you might not care too much.

You should also figure out how working abroad might impact you here in the U.S. Taxes come to mind. If you expect to pay taxes abroad, you should figure out how, if at all, that will affect your U.S. tax returns *before you take the job abroad.* The answer may be positive, negative or neutral depending on where you'll be working, for how long you'll be working abroad, how much you are earning, the terms of any applicable tax treaties, your employer's policies, and so forth. You might even be exempt from U.S. taxation all together.

In addition, when you live and work in a foreign country, that country's laws will apply to you. The laws may be very different, and I mean very different, from our laws.

Educate yourself before you go. If you need help educating yourself, then hire somebody who knows, or a suite of multiple somebodies who collectively know (e.g., lawyers, accountants, financial advisors).

The Good – Gotta Love Some of Those European Countries

Just because foreign laws are very different than our laws doesn't mean the foreign laws are worse than ours. The truth is you might receive more rights working in a foreign country than in the U.S.

Many European countries, for example, have laws that are much more protective of employees than our laws. In some of those countries you might receive "acquired rights" as a matter of law, rights that are unknown in the U.S. Some countries even guarantee you (if you're a resident employee) a government hearing before your employer is able to fire you. If you're laid off or disabled, you might receive required severance pay for a period of time, possibly one or more years.

Guaranteed vacation is also a beauty over there in Europe. Four, five and six weeks of paid vacation are the norm in many places. To some Americans, the Europeans never seem to work – possibly you'll enjoy that lifestyle!

While you gotta love the built-in severance, vacation and employee protection plans of some European nations, it may not all be roses. For example, you might be subject to brutal non-compete clauses in some foreign countries as compared to none or much less stringent ones in California, North Dakota, Oklahoma and other states. Get a lawyer and figure things out before you sign up.

Long Live King Willem-Alexander Claus George Ferdinand!

"Where you going to be living?" I asked.

"Amsterdam!" Dante replied.

"Are you sure you want to work in Amsterdam?"

"Are you kidding me? It's one of the greatest cities in Europe. Centrally located! Great business! Great chocolate!"

"I thought you hate monarchs. They have a King and Queen you know."

"He's a eunuch. She's whatever you call a female eunuch. Totally useless pretty boy and girl figureheads."

"Which you are going to tell everyone once you set up shop there?"

"Only when I'm stoned. They sell it in coffee shops over there you know," Dante replied.

"But never during the weekday," Dante continued. "You know I'm a $2,000-a-suit-guy during business hours!

That's why they pay me the big bucks to tell the Euros how to do things!"

"5 years in jail!"

"What?"

"Say after me: Long live King Willem-Alexander Claus George Ferdinand. Come on, say it."

"Yeah right."

"Five years is the max jail time you can get in Holland if you intentionally insult the Dutch ruler."

"Bull."

"I think you get a year less if you insult Máxima Zorreguieta Cerruti and I am pretty sure, Catharina-Amalia Beatrix Carmen Victoria."

"Who the hell are they?"

"The Dutch Queen and Heir. Could be worse. If you work in Thailand and insult the King there, you might get 15 years behind bars."

The Bad

It pays to know the laws of the nation where you'll be working before you sign up to work there.

Do you like a drink? Maybe fine champagne, or a great port? Maybe a Bloody Mary? Maybe rotgut whiskey?

Drink alcohol in Sudan, and you might wind up with a lashing – yes, you read that correctly, a lashing. In Iran, you could be flogged (that's a lashing) more than seventy times for insulting the Iranian ruler.

And the Truly Ugly

They have great food in Singapore! Malaysian, Chinese, Indian and Indonesian dishes are sold side-by-side at markets throughout Singapore, a true panoply of international cuisine.

But if you use drugs in Singapore, you could be put to death, whereas in the U.S., that same use may be legal, or if not legal, may not result in a prison sentence.

It really pays to know the laws of the nation you'll be working in *before* you sign up to work there.

Things to Remember:

- If you live and work only in the U.S., foreign laws may still affect you.
- If you work abroad, learn how foreign laws affect your working and financial life.
- Sometimes foreign laws can be mighty bad for you, even life threatening!
- On the other hand, sometimes foreign laws can be better for you than our laws.
- Enjoy your time abroad!!

18

Final Things to Remember

And so, our tour of entrepreneurial and executive America ends. I hope you've enjoyed it!

Some final thoughts and themes to reemphasize.

The most important thing to remember: You can get fired. CEOs get fired, CFOs get fired, EVPs get fired, Founders get fired, and so does everyone else on down the organizational chart, all the way to you (and below you too). Negotiate like a CEO and protect yourself with a professional prenuptial agreement, if at all possible. If you can't, or choose not to, at least you now know some of the things that might happen to you in your professional life. Those things might be outstanding! Or, they might be atrocious! Or they may be somewhere in between.

On the outstanding side, CEOs and entrepreneurs often make millions, and so do many at their companies, including hopefully you. Remember the wealth that Xerxes Protective Systems, Inc. C-Suite executives from Chapter 11 experienced when their company sold to an international company. Remember too, the wealth that Claire and the 58 other employees in Chapter 5 garnered when their employer went public.

Claire and the Xerxes Protective Systems C-Suite executives seem to have made it without professional prenuptial agreements. Or maybe they had them, but didn't need them.

On the atrocious side, remember Linda's departure in Chapter 2, Nate and Will Pinot's exits in Chapter 4, CFO Derfy's struggles in Chapter 7, and Cain firing Jeff in Chapter 8. A professional prenuptial agreement would have helped them all.

Linda, Nate, Will, Derfy and Jeff may all tell you six months later that leaving their employer was the best thing that ever happened to them. But the departure might have been a little sweeter, alas a lot sweeter for Linda, with a professional prenuptial agreement negotiated in advance.

And back to Claire and the Xerxes executives: who knows whether others lost out on their good fortune because they were fired at Claire's company or Xerxes before the big event (sale, IPO), and had no protection. Remember, with professional prenuptial protection, you would not lose out.

I don't know whether the Xerxes executives will ever work again, but Claire probably will. There's nothing to say that Claire won't be mistreated where she now works, or in another job that she takes down the road. Even if you and your neighbors, friends, colleagues and mentors have all had great employment experiences sans protection in the past, remember that the next job may be one where things go wrong. It's like those financial advisor warnings: past performance is no guarantee of future success.

Remember to be cold and calculating in your thinking, whether you're thinking about going into a job or, on the other hand, exiting one, or anywhere in between. No matter how much that new job looks like it's perfect for you, no matter how much equity you'll receive, no matter how excited you are, remember to coldly and calculatingly think about whether you should, and/or can, protect yourself.

Of course, if you've been let go, forced out, or downright fired, remember to think coldly and calculatingly about your back-end separation negotiation. If you can laugh all the way to the bank with more money, equity or benefits, who cares that you meet face-to-face to negotiate with the boss who just fired you for incompetence? Remember, the goal is to maximize your return on exit, whatever maximization means for you and whatever reasonable means get you there.

No matter what you're thinking about, whether climbing the corporate ladder, becoming CEO, negotiating an employment or separation agreement or making a job change, remember your trusted and experienced advisors, whoever they are. Besides offering support, good advisors will focus you on cold and calculating business decision making, that is, if you need to be reminded.

Although having fun on the job is not the focus of this book, remember to think about whether entrepreneurial and executive America, corporate America, is right for you. You may not have thought about it, but there's nothing in this book that says entrepreneur and executive America is for you, that it's some type of personal panacea, or anything like that. Back when I had hair on my head and hitchhiked the world,

I met myriad happy people living and working in places that those in entrepreneurial and executive America would probably never want to visit.

If fun on the job means being an executive, think about what you want to run. While the story about Walter Geneva and Butch Haver at the beginning of Chapter 10 illustrates life at the top for the CEO, consider whether you would rather be Walter, CEO of a successful multinational, or Butch, Executive Director of a small non-profit feeding the homeless.

Remember too: There's always professional reincarnation if you're unhappy in your job, or you get the axe. Think of Katarina Nguen and Jim Jeep in Chapter 15. Certainly, there will be easier times in your life and the economic cycle to reincarnate, but the possibility is almost always there.

I realize you may have picked up this book simply looking for an interesting read. Like people who travel for fun and adventure, you sought fun and adventure, or maybe not adventure, but entertainment. If you had a good read, then remember to read my next book … whenever I write it. And remember those laws if you ever do travel abroad: Long Live King Willem-Alexander Clause George Ferdinand!

Afterword - Thanks

Thanks so much to Tamatha (Tammie) Meek who reviewed multiple drafts of my manuscript and offered myriad helpful suggestions.

A special word about Tammie: She is a spectacular lawyer who has worked as "of counsel" at my law firm for years. She is as good as a negotiator for entrepreneurs and executives as you'll find.

But the story I like most about Tammie is the one I call, "Tammie and the Porcelain Goddess." A number of years back, Tammie and I arbitrated a case against a big multinational. The multinational brought in one of its execs from abroad to testify. The witness was literally a porcelain goddess: beautiful translucent skin, lilting enchanting accent, tons of brains, basically the whole package.

Tammie's cross-examination of the porcelain goddess felt like a dinner conversation. Never once did Tammie raise her voice. But she took apart the goddess who eventually wound up conceding that just about everything Tammie suggested on cross was true. It was remarkable.

Around two years later, I ran into the arbitrator who heard the case. "Does that lawyer still work for your firm," he asked. "Yes," I replied.

"She is very talented," the arbitrator responded. "You're a real character. But she, she's a great lawyer."

Thanks to Steven Piser – the biggest pain-in-the-ass of a lawyer and friend one can have – for taking the time to read a draft and offer prescient suggestions. A very big thanks also to Lisa Mammel, a gifted writer and friend, for your very valuable and valued comments.

Thanks too to assistants Valerie Axen, Vicki Sommerdyke and Megan Harper for watching over my law firm while I wrote this book … and to Valerie for bringing years of "adult supervision" to the practice.

I also want to thank all the baristas and other employees who work, or worked at Peet's Coffee in Half Moon Bay, California where I wrote this book. Every one of you was unfailingly friendly whenever I showed up to write. I'm not actually a coffee guy, but rather favor hot chocolate, which barista Kylie always remembered. I realize employee turnover is high at coffee houses, but for whoever is left, I look forward to saying "hello" and showing you what I've written when this book is published.

To my publishers, Lewis Slawsky and Alex Wall at Political Animal Publishing, thanks so much for everything.

One last story, this one about the four people way in the front of this book:

It was an early Saturday morning back in 1964. Oscar and Harry were staying at Pearl's house in Westbury, Long Island, New York. Today was the Bar Mitzvah of the son of their older sister Sarah. Till the day she passed at 96, Sarah was the family's matriarch. And to Sarah, well, the world basically moved for her eldest. There was only one way to get to the Bar Mitzvah: Early.

With plenty of time to spare and with Pearl's son in tow, Oscar and Harry hopped into the car. Oscar was at the wheel (I don't think Harry ever drove Oscar anywhere in the 80+ years each lived.)

Pearl's oldest loved his uncles, and at two, talked up a knowledgeable storm. So, Oscar turned to his nephew and asked how to get to the shul (synagogue). The kid emphatically told his uncles the way … and the uncles loyally followed the directions …. all the way to Jones Beach!

At the shul, Sarah and Pearl were worried, the Jewish worst-case-scenario worry ….

Just in time … Oscar, Harry, and the kid arrived ….

Oscar, most of all, and many other family members (but never Harry) delighted in re-telling the Jones Beach Bar Mitzvah sojourn story for more than 50 years, probably for the last time at the unveiling of Harry's gravestone. Sarah was alive then, and, after laughing once again at her brothers, remembered clear as day waiting that morning in '64: "we thought they had been in an accident," she said.

The only accident Oscar and Harry had had, of course, was trusting a definitive toddler.

Oscar would eventually become an extremely successful Canadian restaurant entrepreneur. Among other successes, he was one of the Colonel's (of Kentucky Fried Chicken fame) earliest franchisees.

Harry, who started his educational career going to a one room schoolhouse in rural Manitoba, would later earn a Ph.D. in economics from MIT. Harry wrote papers on tax policy into his 80s – he lectured at Cambridge University just months before he passed.

Thankfully, Pearl is still going strong – I'm sure she's proud of this book … undoubtedly worried about something … and missing Sarah, Oscar and Harry.